A DIFFERENT KIND OF
LEADER

ACCELERATING PROGRESS
IN A WORLD OF DISRUPTION

JANET POOT

FOREWORD BY BART VAN DER HEIJDEN

RETHINK PRESS

First published in Great Britain 2018
by Rethink Press (www.rethinkpress.com)

Cover image © Shutterstock / Joe Techapanupreeda

Dedicated to the memory
of my beloved Dad.
He was a business leader
who respected the dignity
and supported the aspirations
of vulnerable citizens
in the most racist of societies.

The strong, calm man is always loved and revered.
He is like a shade-giving tree in a thirsty land,
or a sheltering rock in a storm.
James Allen, 1864–1912

.

Contents

Preface   ix

Foreword   xi

Introduction   1

Why this book?   1

The purpose of this book   3

Chapter One: Understanding the External Environment   **7**

External developments   8

   The changing landscape of talent   8

   The speed of things in an interconnected world   13

   The new world of work   17

   Management by algorithm   18

   Geopolitical developments and changes in society   20

False assumptions   25

Opportunities for leaders   28

Summary   30

**Chapter Two: The Changing Face of the Internal
Organisation**   **33**

Changing dynamics within the workforce   34

Flatter organisations and self-managed teams   37

The impact of technology on the workplace   39

The deadline-driven work mode   43

False assumptions   45

Opportunities for leaders   49
Summary   51

**Chapter Three: Leadership Today – the Transitional
Phase of Half Measures**   **53**

Organisational transformations   53
   Organisations anchored in hierarchy and control   54
   Organisations anchored in management by objectives   55
   Organisations anchored in empowerment   56
   Organisations anchored in self-management   58
Leadership in transition – the risk of half measures   59
Half measures in a personal context   60
   The devil lies in authenticity   60
   Leaders act on the premise of 'more' instead of
   'different'   63
Half measures in strategic business conduct   65
   Indecisiveness   65
   Common examples of poor decision making   66
   Defining the context   68
   Recruitment of talent – a shift to broader diversity 71
Questions for leaders   73
Summary   74

Chapter Four: Preparing for Change   **77**

Leaders   77
On the eve of self-management   82
Professional identity – think purpose   83
   Role   84
   Exercise: Create your role on a flipchart   86
   Mapping your Role   87
Be consistent, not predictable   90
   Choice of words   91

Your choices96

Energy management above time management99

Applying energy management in our networks100

Stakeholder Wheel103

Stakeholder partnership plan104

Summary106

Chapter Five: On the Job109

Diversity abroad, sameness at home?110

The power of observation115

Role model in a time of disruption121

The use of big data123

Image and reputation management126

Mindset129

Moral leadership – the three-way principle133

Summary139

Chapter Six: Teams Today – the Most Common Limitations141

The over-analysed team144

An overload of unchannelled co-operation146

Restrictive problem solving and decision making149

The missing ingredient – empathy151

Summary154

Chapter Seven: Modern Team and Intergenerational Leadership155

Leadership of fluid teams156

Intergenerational leadership168

Respect168

Understanding the differences170

Opportunities for leaders173

Summary   176

Chapter Eight: When the Going Gets Tough   **179**

Momentum – what is it and how do you build it?   180
    Guiding principles   180
When change becomes overwhelming   181
When opposition mounts   184
    Expect detours   184
    Create a list of potential risks   185
    Reconnect based on curiosity   185
    Reframe your message and approach   185
    Increase your presence and communication   186
    Accept that you have supporters and opponents 186
Using your personal reset button   187
    Reflect, Record, Rehearse, Remember, Reproduce 188
    Red flags   189
    Retain your professional conduct   189
Summary   190

Postscript   **193**

Acknowledgements   **195**

The Author   **197**

Preface

Constant innovation across all industries has become the major force determining an organisation's future success. Pressure on business leaders to lead the change necessary in our complex and dynamic world has never been as high as it is today. A different kind of leader is called for – but do we know what this means, and how to put our understanding of leadership into effective action to successfully achieve our goals?

In *A Different Kind of Leader* Janet invites us – the leaders of today and tomorrow – to join her on a journey as she navigates us through the eight chapters of her book to, in her own words, '…fast-track progress in your company and position'. The power of the book lies in the fact that Janet bases her deep insights and practical learnings on personal experience and extensive research gained from years of professional practice as a leader, business entrepreneur, and inspiring leadership consultant operating internationally and across all business sectors.

Her book offers a fresh, stimulating, and innovative approach to leadership as she guides the reader through the forces that are transforming the global economy and accelerating industry disruption, calling for organisational transformation and leadership change. She shares her thoughts on the profound economic and social implications of these forces, the complexities relevant to organisations and their leadership, and the urgent need to prepare for transformation and leadership change in a world of disruption.

Janet enables the reader to use models and exercises to explore their own leadership styles, learn how to develop the right leadership qualities, and transition from understanding to effective action, to become dynamic and strategic leaders using constructive influence.

The book is filled with valuable ideas on how to prepare for organisational and leadership transition, and to bring about meaningful change in a fast-paced world. The reader is left energised, motivated and prepared to take on the challenges they face. It makes for powerful reading.

Lana van der Spiegel-Breytenbach

Lana van der Spiegel-Breytenbach has lived in South Africa and several European countries. She has worked in both the public and the private sector as a lawyer, as a senior diplomat in London and Paris, a specialist in the global intellectual property industry, and more recently as an advisor to large global corporations. She has held senior positions and directorships at South African, Finnish, American and UK multinationals.

Foreword

I got to know Janet Poot at the RAI a number of years ago and we have always remained in contact, whether this was in the context of consultancy, coaching or management training programmes. Janet is highly appreciated by our organisation, thanks to her personal engagement, professional expertise and structured approach, all combined with her entrepreneurial and international experience.

I certainly see the relevance of *A Different Kind of Leader* in my role. My influence is no longer determined by my position or title. More than ever before, it is linked to adapting to changing needs and applying specific interpersonal skills in an unpredictable world. I began my career at the RAI as a trainee and now, on the Board of Directors, I have a key role to fulfil in facilitating ongoing change. I completed an executive programme for leadership development at IESE Business School of Barcelona where I met many international executives. Through my contacts with them I have discovered that we all face similar challenges, regardless of our sectors or cultures. This confirms the findings as described in this book.

A Different Kind of Leader is a real page-turner, with so many teasers that you just want to keep on reading. I was particularly struck by the importance of being role- rather than task-driven, facilitating fluid teams for greater synergy, and one of the biggest eye-openers is the recognisable risk in many organisations of seeking safety in half measures.

We see the world around us evolving at a furious speed. New players and generations come unannounced and disrupt the market. They are driven by technological developments and appear to outplay the competition effortlessly. We must stay ahead of this and for this reason we are building an organisation with a new culture and operating model, equipped to capitalise on external developments faster.

We expect to be faced by challenges. Staying ahead does, however, require a different way of thinking and acting. The future of our business is intrinsically linked to working in a data-driven environment: how will we deal with this? Being prepared requires change. We will, therefore, work together in achieving more innovation, a new structure and culture, supported by a leadership team that embraces the essence of *A Different Kind of Leader*.

Bart van der Heijden
Director at RAI Amsterdam, International Convention Centre

Introduction

Why this book?

There is no shortage of books on the topic of leadership, so a fair question may be why have I dedicated my time to writing another one? It is the volume of books on offer that inspired me to cut through the maze of theories, tips, and tools to provide insights, different perspectives, and concrete choices for leaders in a business world that is intolerant of more of the same.

These are ultra-dynamic times, and every person in business around the world is, to some extent or another, faced with a form of transition. This may be from one organisational structure to another, a changeover to new processes, a shift to a different marketing approach or policies, or a merger with another organisation – these are just some examples of a virtually endless list of circumstances that test our resilience, adaptability and resourcefulness as well as our commitment to progress.

An increasing level of complexity exists both within companies and in the external business environment, where unexpected and disruptive developments are rapidly becoming the norm. This unpredictable world is exciting for some companies and daunting for others, depending on their ability to adapt to the speed of change. It is this quality that plays a big role in determining the lifespan of a company, making adaptability a big 'must-have' attribute for senior managers.

There is no doubt that the pressures on business leaders today have increased as they are expected to meet an ever-changing set of expectations and master a long list of skills. These expectations include being influential speakers, visionary leaders, inspirational drivers of innovation and change, focused thinkers, charismatic networkers and, last but not least, culturally intelligent negotiators. The summary of 'must haves' looked quite different at companies that chose a strategy of consolidation during the recent credit crisis – the longest economic downturn since the 1930s. A defensive management style became more prevalent, and more former chief finance officers were selected for CEO positions than in preceding decades.

Can leaders retain or increase their relevance in a world in which traditional business models are losing ground and innovation is driven more and more by cross-functional teams and knowledge centres? To this we must add the rapid development of smart devices, artificial intelligence and IT solutions, which are shaping companies and cross-border digital traffic such as e-commerce. This is a world in which e-commerce continues to grow faster than the traditional trade in goods and services.

Leadership has, in fact, never been more important than it is today. It is not about doing more, rather it is about removing counterproductive obstacles and inconsistencies, adding value where relevant, and making clear choices in order to excel as a different kind of leader.

The purpose of this book

A Different Kind of Leader puts you and your role as a leader centre stage as we address current developments, dilemmas and opportunities. My objective is for you to gain practical insights to fast-track progress in your company and position, and feel energised to put these important insights into practice without delay. This time of disruption may prove to be the right time for you to stand out in certain areas or renew a specific approach, skill or competency to become more effective.

This is not an instructional 'how to' manual, offering an over-simplification of the business environment. Neither does it describe the best business practice in any given circumstance as no two company cultures, backgrounds or objectives are the same. However, I will take a practical and experience-based approach as I share useful insights with you, including exercises so that you can assess what to do differently to achieve the end result you have in mind.

The content of *A Different Kind of Leader* has been driven by my own professional background and expertise, and by current business developments. After working in employment, I established an international marketing company in my mid-twenties and became an entrepreneur who thrived in the dynamic world of airport marketing. Leadership took on a whole new meaning when I expanded to different countries with branch offices abroad and a multicultural workforce. Eye-opening experiences and a fair share of tough and humorous situations brought me much fulfilment and a thorough understanding of what it takes to succeed as an international entrepreneur. Many years later I prepared in the USA for a new dimension to my career and established a second company to focus on international leadership and consultancy. This area of expertise has brought me clients from every continent.

However different cultures and the issues at hand may be, leaders across the globe face many of the same core challenges.

Let me now take you through the contents of *A Different Kind of Leader*. Our journey will start in the external environment where we will look at developments that are changing our world at a rapid pace. Succeeding through being a different kind of leader begins with an understanding of the external influences that impact on people's professional lives and circumstances. We will then observe behavioural patterns within organisation today, taking a bird's-eye view of key developments across the board. We will also zoom in on false assumptions and discuss alternatives.

Having a clear picture of the external environment and internal organisation, we will then bring the leader into the picture. We will discuss leadership today and address in practical terms the meaning of half-measures, as well as their pitfalls. Moving into the world of a different kind of leadership begins with preparing to be a different kind of leader. We will address topics such as role and positioning, communication, choices and energy management. We will highlight current challenges and competencies that will help you be a role model, which include image and reputation management. What does this entail and how does one achieve it in this world of disruption?

Leaders lead teams, and teams, too, are in transition. What do they look like? Before we can identify opportunities to lead differently, we must have a good understanding of how teams function today and be aware of their greatest challenges. We will then be ready to apply a different kind of leadership to build teams that are ready for ongoing change. Leading modern teams and achieving intergenerational diversity are two vital skills that will differentiate leaders from their peers.

Finally, we will acknowledge the existence of open and hidden resistance and share ideas on how a leader can build resilience to maintain momentum and progress. Hurdles can be discouraging, but they also signal you're moving beyond familiar and predictable terrain.

Welcome on board. I hope you will enjoy reading and reflecting on *A Different Kind of Leader.*

To read without reflecting is like
eating without digesting.
Edmund Burke

1

Understanding the External Environment

The world is changing very fast.
Big will not beat small anymore.
It will be the fast beating the slow.
Rupert Murdoch, CEO of 21st Century Fox

There can be no better place to gain an understanding of our business circumstances and performance than in the external environment. Leaders seeking improvements and opportunities first from within the organisation reinforce an inward focus and then tend to deliver, at best, an efficiency gain.

In times of uncertainty, many organisations are inclined to focus primarily on internal improvements. Therefore it is not surprising that, for many companies, 'efficiency' ranks in the top three key performance indicators in times of crisis. Focusing on what can be done quicker and cheaper based on quantifiable data is an exercise that can be done with a level of routine and certainty regardless of external turbulence and complexities. Unfortunately, this approach can slow a company down strategically.

To stay clear of premature introspective inclinations, we need to move into the wider world. It so often tends to be visited in reactive or autopilot mode as a result of a deadline-driven life and work style.

External developments

It would be easy to fill page after page with every type of notable development. My choice is to highlight four current external developments that I believe call for a strategic response.

The changing landscape of talent

Businesses across the globe struggle to attract and retain the best employees to face intensifying global competition. Add a big dose of talent mobility to this scarcity, and the result is a patchy landscape of talent resembling Emmental cheese.

What we see in practice in an integrated world with innovation at its core is a growing need for information and brainpower to move around freely. Innovation depends on this mobility and employees believe their growth should transcend companies and borders. This talent mobility for innovation on a global scale has led to the validity of non-compete clauses in labour contracts, which protect a company's most confidential data and knowledge, being challenged. They are no longer considered by judges in many countries to be automatically binding. Millennials (born 1981–2001) in particular believe that if they cannot make a difference or get ahead, then they won't waste their time in the wrong position or organisation. This generation has an intrinsic desire to move to greener pastures.

Many industrial countries across the globe are facing a static, shrinking and/or ageing workforce. These changing demographics are having a considerable impact on economies that depend on having the means, human and automated, to meet their growth objectives. To offset the impact of an overstretched workforce, it is expected that the number of robots worldwide will show a steady increase in all sectors. Immigration will not suffice to solve the steep demand for hands and brains in markets such as China, Japan and Germany.

For example, in Japan a shortage of farmers and a reliance on ageing farmers who continue to work into their eighties has led to the introduction of robotic farming. To increase Japanese food self-sufficiency, agricultural machine manufacturers are now working on producing smart driverless tractors that are able to work the challenging ground of rice paddies. The future could see farmers in Japan relieved of all physical labour while their robo-tractors do the heavy work, from ploughing to harvesting.

Whereas the growth of the working population used to be a good gauge of economic progress, it is now widely believed that the number of robots used in industries will become the new measuring tool to determine growth potential and productivity.

In all regions, governments are seeking new strategies to develop their workforces to meet the demands of our century. European Commissioner for the Digital Single Market and Vice President of the European Commission, Andrus Ansip, stated that Europe could face a shortage of more than 800,000 skilled ICT workers by 2020. The skills gap today is significant, and one may argue that artificial intelligence has come just in time to tackle global challenges in diverse sectors. What we need is a strategy to ensure workers are trained to use and work alongside robotic equipment, and leaders who understand how best to use and develop the talents of their human resources.

The technology of machine learning is a high-ranking requirement for companies dealing with an unprecedented volume of data. Machine learning basically means that computers are given the ability to learn on their own without being specifically programmed to collect and analyse certain information. Reinforcement learning means that machines learn tasks based on trial and error, but machines may soon be able to learn from human demonstration, described as imitation learning. Whatever the form of machine learning may be, using this technology means that robots will be able to carry out many more tasks.

Machine learning is a topic that some organisations prefer to let rest for the time being. Others are aware that it will make routine jobs performed by average knowledge workers superfluous as they will be automatable and performed faster. It is to be expected that the impact of this algorithmic technology on jobs will be on most companies' agendas worldwide within a couple of years. Executives will experience the need to understand and use artificial intelligence themselves as part of their daily work.

The world of machine learning will have an impact on education. Certain studies will disappear as graduates find they have to compete with machines. Vocational training is gaining importance in many countries as a result of a widened gap between the skills and knowledge of students and the talents companies are seeking. Being educated with the workplace in mind would bridge this gap and ensure a better match between credentials and demand. Research shows that MBAs are beginning to lose their golden appeal as employers look for other qualifications. There is already a significant shortfall of available talent in the field of big data analysis and coding. New recruits today are expected to have specific skills that include understanding the impact of technological developments on businesses, digital and finance management, building diverse networks and seeing the big picture in relation to complex problems.

It is not surprising, therefore, that education systems worldwide are being reformed. Yet Sir Ken Robinson, author and educator, challenges the world to be more radical in the choices it makes, to educate its children differently. His opinion is that the world's education systems should not be improved but revolutionised to cultivate creativity and acknowledge multiple types of intelligence. Sir Ken Robinson compares the current education system to an industrial environment, making the comparison between the linear education model and factories where conformity is the norm. I believe that the risk of eroding creativity also lurks in traditionally led organisations today.

Cybersecurity is an area of growing concern for both governments and companies. It has become easy to launch Distributed Denial of Service attacks. These destructive cyber-attacks use multiple compromised computers and internet connections to flood the victim's system with an excessive volume of data that can paralyse an organisation's business. Cyber-attacks have led to an emerging area of talent that will be increasingly sought-after: cybersecurity experts who are trained to secure organisations' defences.

The number of vacancies for certified ethical hackers, also known as 'white hat hackers' or 'white hats', is likely to surge. These hackers use the same knowledge and tools as malicious hackers in a legitimate way to penetrate systems as they test an organisation's IT security and identify vulnerabilities. IT staff then use the results of the penetration tests to repair weaknesses and reduce the risk factors.

Flatter organisational structures and changing business models are on the rise, and this is attributed to closer ties and frequent communication between business partners across the globe. This has an impact on how talents are developed and the expectations of employees.

Finding the right candidates will require HR to use very different selection and assessment methods, which will include new technology in various phases of the recruitment process. Not only are organisations able to use machines to read and preselect résumés, the use of artificial intelligence is also available to job seekers. Application bots will help them to find vacancies that are best suited to their skills, and will also generate and send well-formulated letters based on the specifications of the vacancy. We will see a growing volume of applications in circulation, and artificial intelligence will be used to screen the letters, resulting in machines speaking to machines in the initial phase of candidate and job search processes. HR managers will also be faced with changing expectations as many candidates will not be seeking a nine to five job or fixed contract.

Flexibility and a new mindset will be essential to acquire the best talents. Some of the workforce may want to work on-demand and companies will have to accommodate these needs. Robotics will eliminate certain jobs, and companies must prepare for a policy that ensures the upgrading of skills and upward mobility. Moving employees higher up the value chain of human knowledge and skills is steadily becoming a main priority. There is no doubt that timing is a challenge. In every part of the world new technology is becoming available. Preparing for revolutionary change in the workplace cannot be delayed.

Social media is another area that influences the landscape of talent. As businesses compete for talent, it is not uncommon for them to oversell the opportunities they offer to new recruits. This quick-fix solution can, however, backfire and lead to an early talent drain if companies make unrealistic promises which a disappointed former employee shares on social media. The former employee may be blamed for lack of loyalty, but responsibility lies with the company for not managing expectations or living up to promises it made to new employees. Excellent corporate reputation management must, therefore, be considered a key activity for companies in the context of talent acquisition and retention.

These global talent challenges offer many opportunities if seen through a wider lens.

The speed of things in an interconnected world

Reflect for a minute on things you are able to do so much faster than a year ago. How much more data do you receive every day, for example from your fitness tracker? Do you have a smart doorbell that allows you to see who is at the door even if you are not home? Or are you an early adopter of the Amazon Key allowing you to give secured access to couriers to deliver your parcels into your home, while you watch the delivery as it happens or afterwards on video?

More than 20,000 smart electronic products were launched at the global tech show, CES, in January 2018. The smart home took central stage as companies competed to control our homes and appliances through their voice assistance technology. Such exponential growth of next-generation innovations will be reflected in the increase of the global market for the internet of things. Putting all our appliances online so that we can access them remotely may seem a logical step to becoming even more efficient and having more data at our disposal, but one of the consequences of this development is a significant increase in the need for cybersecurity. As our online vulnerability increases, cyber-security insurance is likely to be considered as important as having house and car insurance.

An example of risks linked to smart appliances is an artificially intelligent vacuum cleaner. This vacuum cleaner collects customer data that it picks up as it moves around the home. Its manufacturer has stated it would consider selling this data, which may include information on other appliances, Wi-Fi connections, home layout plans, and the home owner's behavioural patterns.

When it comes to the tech sector, the world is a global village. Products and services penetrate people's daily lives from locations that could be thousands of miles away. FinTech, HealthTech, LegalTech are all here to stay. Research findings published by the European Trade Union Institute (2016) highlight the disruption caused by the Fourth Industrial Revolution, but each new revolution brings opportunities too. We will see the creation of jobs and new sectors as products and services evolve. Existing jobs will change and some will shift to other regions. Therefore, the speed of an interconnected world need not be seen as a threat, but as an opportunity.

Every daily newspaper, business journal or news app has something to report that indicates 'this could be significant'. My moment today was an article on the use of facial-recognition technology by a lecturer in China to help him determine the students' level of interest in his lectures. The data may record at what point students lose interest, struggle to understand or disengage from the lecture. This instant feedback can be used to improve an approach, content or method of delivery.

The pace of innovation has had an impact on the lifespan of companies that, statistically, is proven to be shorter today. Disrupters are not simply aggressive competitors who steal market share; their business model is different and disrupts how business is done.

The tech giants – Apple, Google/Alphabet, Microsoft, Amazon, Facebook – have an enormous advantage that enables them to be potential disrupters in any sector. They control the world's flow of information, and the volume of data that they have amassed on customer needs and behavioural patterns allows them to identify real opportunities and offer services that outclass those provided by market leaders in any given sector. They have search data telling them not only what people are looking for, but also what people cannot find.

Amazon sent shockwaves through the aviation industry when it launched its own cargo airline to transport its products. It managed to establish a fleet of approximately thirty cargo planes within one year, which was unprecedented.

This demonstrates that there could be many more surprises to come from the big players in the tech sector.

Let's look at an example in the field of LegalTech.

CHANGE IN THE LEGAL WORLD

A LegalTech company, established in 2008, reports it has provided digital legal services to 20 million people. Their services include 'do it yourself' websites where legal documents can be downloaded; websites where clients and lawyers meet; and a platform for the providers of software that automates legal procedures. General counsels of large companies are not likely to use online marketplaces, but LegalTech is expected to rock the foundations of small to medium size legal firms in multiple countries.

Authority linked to the control of international data and communication flows is unprecedented. I was struck by the term 'Facebookism' recently. Facebook users are actually Facebook's product. As Timotheus Höttges, CEO of Deutsche Telekom, said, 'There isn't anything for free. The moment something is free, you are the product.' Every Facebook 'like' is recorded, analysed and made available to those who will pay for highly segmented marketing information. Possessing and using so much data regarding citizens' social status, concerns, biases and preferences can have far-reaching political consequences.

And what about consumer behaviour? Here we see speed too. Consumers have never had a greater choice of products and services at their fingertips, and they are discovering these products and services at a record-breaking speed. This is mainly thanks to word of mouth via social media platforms. Businesses cannot afford to ignore the influence of digital crowds. In fact, they need to take digital crowds into account when branding a product or service.

To summarise, we can say that fast technological advancement requires companies to be resilient and able to adjust quickly to external influences and disruptive innovators. Our interconnected world is filled with opportunity and surrounded by different forms of complexity. Distance in many respects is becoming negligible. The use of bots means that time zones no longer dictate the speed of a response to consumers.

Is this digital revolution exciting or daunting? Positive or negative? The answer will differ from person to person. It is certainly daunting and negative for any business seeking to deter competition or increase stability.

The new world of work

It would be virtually impossible for changes to occur everywhere except in labour markets. Governments in developed economies are struggling to find answers to what is perceived by many to be an undesirable move towards more and more flexibility in employer-employee relationships. Businesses are engaging freelancers at a higher rate than ever before. Therefore, flexible work contracts are on the rise, and these include zero-hour contracts that do not guarantee a minimum amount of work. Less job security, more part-time work and looser ties between employers and employees are changing the landscape of economies that were once characterised by contingent work.

The gig economy, a term coined in the USA for an environment in which temporary positions and on-demand contracts for short-term engagements are commonplace, continues to gain ground in Europe too. The number of flex workers has shown a steep increase in multiple European countries that simultaneously show a decrease in the number of flex contracts that transition to permanent contracts. There is much debate on the advantages and perils of this new world of work. At this point in time insufficient research has been done for conclusive results. Early signs are that governments will shift to accommodate the need for flexibility and entrepreneurship while also claiming more benefits or protection for freelancers.

Robotics and artificial intelligence are disrupting industries across the globe. The word algorithm is now part of everyday business vocabulary, and a topic attracting much attention is algorithmic management.

Management by algorithm

Ride-hailing company Uber is a clear example of a working environment managed entirely by algorithms. An automated system controls all communication with the drivers, from the minute drivers log in remotely to when they have completed a job. There is no human interference behind the scenes and no interaction between the drivers and a manager. Digital messages control each assignment and automated corrective measures, including job terminations, are taken if data shows work is not satisfactory. This is a level of control and accuracy a human being could not deliver.

There are many other areas where algorithmic management techniques offer accuracy in planning and execution, and provide supervision, too. This is the world of data-ism; a world where authority moves from humans to computer algorithms. This is not without concern or unrest among many workers. So how far does one go?

The new world of work is a complex one. Leaders must focus on structures and processes that facilitate using the right technology for the fastest, most convenient and best quality services. This should go hand in hand with establishing a workplace that retains a human touch and positive climate.

And then we see increased mobility. LinkedIn, Facebook and Glassdoor are examples of networking tools that enable people to monitor the market for new job opportunities instantly, and these opportunities could be local or international. This is not new, but in this digital age, work can be done from any location. Therefore, freelancers have equal opportunities to fulfil projects around the world.

Companies will continue to expand into new markets and shift or increase their scope to (include) new regions. Communication channels have changed rapidly and contacts across borders are established at lower functional levels. Therefore, the new world of work is one that puts intercultural communication and understanding, and all underlying skills such as negotiating with overseas partners, centre stage. It is a changing environment where companies compete more on how they sell than what they sell. Traditional functions are not sustainable. Lines of communication if drawn on a chart would resemble a mesmerising pattern of intertwining roads.

Does this new world of work demand a different communication or leadership style? Definitely. Don't underestimate the importance of having a policy regarding trust, communication, authority, and career advancement for different types of contractual workers. Without a policy or guidelines, leaders may demonstrate inconsistencies in their communication and conduct, rely too heavily on 'gut feeling', underutilise talent and fail to build sufficient engagement within the organisation. We also need human leadership to determine the extent to which algorithmic techniques are applied and to which purpose. The context has changed, and so must the game plan.

Geopolitical developments and changes in society

Technology made large populations possible;
large populations now make technology indispensable.
Joseph Wood Krutch

Globalisation remains a topic of broad current interest. It generates heated debates and conflicting opinions regarding its future. A wave of protectionism and anti-globalisation associated with Donald Trump's America First policy, the British vote to exit the EU and the rise of populism have kept the topic of globalisation in the spotlight. But I strongly believe that globalisation will not be reversed.

Globalisation describes a process by which national
and regional economies, societies and cultures have
become integrated through the global network of trade,
communication, immigration and transportation.
FT Lexicon

This doesn't sound like a process that can be sent on a sabbatical. As long as economic and societal inequality prevails, support for open economies will shrink. This may result in protectionism, changes in foreign policies, and ultimately even a new world order, but globalisation will not come to a standstill.

Governments are working on bilateral trade agreements and negotiations with new partners. This increased activity in trade negotiations and deals from Europe to Canada to Asia to Latin America is steaming ahead, regardless of the USA government's stance on multilateral trading partnerships.

Developments in the field of financial globalisation changed after the 2007–2008 credit crisis. What seemed to be an unrestrainable trend within banking was reined in and cross-border capital flows were heavily restricted. But reversal was not possible. FinTech is evidence of how technology in the financial sector will not be restricted to the confinements of national borders. The world is showing increased interest in the use of digital currencies, known as cryptocurrencies, of which bitcoin was the first. Japan is one of the largest markets for trading bitcoin, where this payment method is possible at hundreds of retailers and restaurants.

The operating system used for bitcoin transactions is the blockchain – a cheap and secure way of facilitating international trade. In simple terms, each transaction is a block linked to the chain by computers providing a permanent record.

The world deserves better management or regulatory models, and an inclusive approach to have capital flow to where it is most needed. Without fundamental change, inequality will lead to more income insecurity and decreased social welfare. These are two ingredients that contribute to frustrated individuals wanting to do whatever it takes to undermine liberal Western societies. It is within this context of societal concern, political turmoil and an increased sense of distrust that social polarisation and populism have found fertile ground. And it is in such volatile environments that differences are not respected or valued sufficiently and stereotyping and labelling are used in an almost alarming measure.

Companies operate in the midst of such dynamics and may underestimate the extent to which the exterior and interior of the company are interconnected. External sentiments spill over into the business climate, and there's a necessity for executives to demonstrate the values and principles the company stands for.

Give some thought to stereotyping in your business surroundings. Do you ever recognise the signs of pigeonholing of generations, clients, other departments or regional offices?

The fast digitalisation of the economy and advancement of innovation are reflected in an accelerated way of life. Cities are growing and multiplying, and they are able to sustain such expansion only thanks to innovation. According to the UN, by 2030 there will be forty-one cities with a population of more than ten million people, compared to twenty-eight cities of that size today. More people will require more speed, and developments in social media, robotics, artificial intelligence, and the internet of things will make sure that speed is maintained.

We have discussed how artificial intelligence is revolutionising industries. It is also challenging societies to consider regulation regarding its progression and use. Prominent leaders in the tech industry are urging governments to take proactive measures for the sake of transparency and regulation in a world that must be safeguarded from unpredictable robot-driven actions and the development of autonomous weapons.

Western societies are ageing and retirement ages are rising. What does this mean in a business context? We now have multigenerational workforces which are often described as highly challenging. I am surprised by the negative titles of books on this topic, particularly those that refer to collisions between generations, the widening gap and the great divide. My viewpoint is different. I believe that sameness blocks creativity and hampers innovation. We require that wider lens to see and value differences to generate synergy – more on this topic in Chapter Seven.

Let's now take a closer look at international political developments. Russia's annexation of Crimea, the UK's vote for Brexit, the election of Donald Trump, increased tensions in relations with North Korea as its missile and cyberattack programmes continue to evolve, and Islamic State's war on free democratic societies are just a few examples of developments that have had a ripple effect across continents. The USA's Western allies no longer consider the USA to be the leader of the free world. China's 2017 launch of the strategic 'One Belt One Road' initiative has shifted the world's attention to the Pacific. This far-reaching infrastructure project is intended to link Asia to Europe making Eurasia the new global power centre. 2017 marked the opening of a new rail freight route linking China to Europe. The train took eighteen days to cross seven countries before arriving in London. China's ambition is to renew the Silk Road and use railways, harbours, airports, dams and pipelines to create the world's largest platform for economic, social and cultural co-operation.

Geopolitics affect international businesses, and here's the choice I believe organisations face: to conduct business as usual across borders and react to barriers that arise in international trade relations, or proactively pursue the most promising business ventures by introducing and working within a tailor-made international corporate foreign policy. In the first situation, businesses rely on past successes and politicians' foreign policy as a guideline. In the second situation, businesses become more knowledgeable of local circumstances and more consistent and influential as they respond to geopolitical developments and sensitivities.

Companies could benefit greatly from having a corporate foreign policy for each country or region of operation that respects the parameters of legal, economic and political agreements, but sets out in proactive terms how business will be conducted in a culturally, socially and politically intelligent manner. A measure of our success is not how we cope in challenging environments but how we as leaders help our staff build alliances based on trust, mutual gain and synergy between all stakeholders. Without a policy, leaders depend too heavily on the ability of individuals to manoeuvre skilfully in unpredictable environments.

Finally, our societies are confronted with the prevalence of fake news. Information spreads through social media channels in a manner that takes us either closer to or further away from the truth. It has proven as easy to spread misinformation as it is to post fact-based news, and this can have a detrimental effect on the reputations of organisations and individuals. High-profile companies have been confronted with fake advertisements placed on their behalf or fake announcements regarding interest groups that they are said to support. In the last quarter of 2017, Facebook testified that about 200 million of its 2.3 billion users were fake. Twitter testified that its fake accounts and spammers were estimated to be over 16 million.

For all citizens there is a growing need to verify the trustworthiness of information.

False assumptions

We have looked at the external environment and highlighted four major developments that have an impact on the role of leaders. Now let's dismiss two assumptions I believe are capable of undermining our success.

Assumption 1: It is OK to be less culturally sensitive in a world that is more interconnected and fast paced.

This is an assumption that I have heard above all in the context of business dealings abroad. Initiating negotiations with a foreign partner may be considered challenging enough without having to get the etiquette right. For some managers, respecting different values, styles of communication and traditions are 'optional extras' they do not have time for. Some may say, 'Surely we can skip the frills and get the job done?' or 'They need our business so it's time for them to adjust to our approach'. I have noticed that these statements are often used to justify a lost opportunity.

Yes, the world is more interconnected, but also more complex and diverse. Succeeding in this environment requires more cultural intelligence, not less, especially when dealing with different kinds of complexities and sensitivities. Communicating and leading successfully across the globe have never been more important.

You may have trading partners or suppliers who work in multiple countries and have merged with or acquired businesses in different parts of the world. Despite their international image and global business dealings, they tend to retain a sense of national pride, treasuring their roots and appreciating what makes their cultural background unique. If you consider how they market themselves, it is likely you will discover that their cultural heritage features in their corporate identity. Therefore, it would be a lost opportunity *not* to respect the cultural qualities that are valued by your business partner. It does not take much effort and ensures that you shift your attention to the interests and wellbeing of the person with whom you are seeking to build a fruitful relationship.

Effective personal skills and conduct, a suitable approach for each setting and valuable interaction can provide the creativity that digital and virtual worlds cannot. Getting it right and enjoying this aspect of business is where I believe you will capitalise most on business potential.

Here's my version of a much better assumption: the more skilled you are at communicating with other cultures, the more effective you will be as a negotiator abroad and as a leader back home. I will elaborate on this point in Chapter Five.

Assumption 2: Turbulence and uncertainty warrant a shorter-term focus.

When unexpected events occur and the business feels the effects of uncertainty or threatening developments, it is not uncommon to see management teams tighten control and even micromanage projects. They will also want to demonstrate strength by speaking about solutions to problems and the need to respond swiftly to new external circumstances. KPI (key performance indicator) 'efficiency' climbs in importance as it is tangible, results are measurable and can be produced quickly. I call this the 'Efficiency Comfort Zone' (ECZ).

When the ECZ becomes well-established, efficiency is then scrutinised in more areas and the results are either celebrated or disliked. It can be a fun and secure place to be. Unless redundancies are involved, decisions that increase efficiency can be taken relatively quickly, the decision makers' influence increases and poor business practices may be revealed.

What is wrong with this? Well, uncertainty and disruptions in the external environment won't go away if the organisation spends valuable leadership time focusing on doing the same (or more) in less time or by using fewer resources. Another risk is that an ECZ creates new patterns in how senior managers think and work. When the efficiency agenda is given priority, it limits creativity in crucial areas of the company.

Of course, the Efficiency Comfort Zone is intended to be a temporary situation, but undoing a pattern is not easy. We do not want the most senior leaders to reside here for too long. They should be short-term visitors to the efficiency agenda, not its owners. It can take time for senior leaders to shift back to setting direction and leading effectively, involving their talented employees and creating the right balance between an inward and outward focus. A short-term focus delivers short-term results that do not necessarily bring about sustainable progress.

If leaders set clear objectives and take the right decisions, their teams will have a natural intolerance of inefficiency.

A long-term focus is crucial, as well as a framework that reduces risks on the one hand and allows for surprising occurrences on the other. It is outside of any comfort zone where real progress is achieved. It can feel good to solve problems, but the more often leaders find themselves solving problems, the greater the need to ask themselves whether they should really be acting as professional trouble shooters. That role is a far cry from becoming influential in setting the agenda and facilitating change.

Opportunities for leaders

The next logical step is to reflect on what we as leaders need to do to capitalise on all this external activity. It is time to study diverse areas of focus that would add value to a leader's agenda.

Responding to external factors

AREA OF FOCUS	EXAMPLES OF STATEMENTS TO CONSIDER	✓/✗
Talent scarcity and mobility	• Your company's policies for talent acquisition and retention are driven by external developments	
	• Talent related processes are dynamic and involve different departments	
	• The promise made to new employees matches reality and helps to attract the right people	
Global digitalisation	• Your company's policy is 'plan ahead for further digitalisation' as opposed to 'adapt as needed'	
	• Senior management is well-informed about innovation and the significance of technological advances for the business	

AREA OF FOCUS	EXAMPLES OF STATEMENTS TO CONSIDER	✓/✗
Customer needs and behaviour	• Your business has a thorough understanding of your customers' needs and behaviour	
	• Knowledge of customers' needs and behaviour are gained less through internal processes (e.g. customer journey or experience mapping) and more in the external environment in direct contact with customers	
New world of work	• You have a clear understanding of what this means for your company	
	• Your company has made a conscious choice between a homogeneous and differential approach for all parties involved in the work force	
	• Mobility is seen as an opportunity and not a threat	
Changes in society: demographic, behavioural, social and geopolitical	• You have given consideration to what you as a leader could do differently to ensure that your organisation is ready to accommodate and benefit from changes in society	
Diversity in all international business dealings	• Intercultural skills are as high on your company's agenda as the bottom-line results forecast for each stakeholder	

This table can be downloaded at http://www.jpcint.com/publications

Please use the blank cell to add any other area of focus based on your own business situation. Then put a tick or cross next to each statement to indicate if it is/is not applicable to you/your organisation.

Now select three areas you wish to focus on, basing your choice on what you know now. It is not necessary at this stage to go into any form of internal analysis. By selecting these topics, you have chosen to do any of the following for each of them:

- Observe processes in practice to establish the current relevance and importance of this topic
- Introduce the topic for policy and strategic purposes
- Challenge others
- Promote this topic internally
- Study this topic further
- Translate it into a key success factor (KSF)
- Build a reputation in this field
- Demonstrate its importance by setting a clear example to others

Summary

We started our journey in the dynamic external environment by studying four developments that continue to bring rapid change:

- The changing landscape of talent
- The speed of things in an interconnected world
- The new world of work
- Geopolitical developments and changes in society

We addressed two false assumptions: 'It is OK to be less culturally sensitive in a world that is more interconnected and fast paced' and 'Turbulence and uncertainty warrant a shorter-term focus'.

You have also highlighted your top three priorities. Keeping these in mind as you read on, you will be able to gain more ideas as to what you could do differently to be in sync with the evolving external transformations concerning your priorities.

We will now move on to the internal environment.

2

The Changing Face of the Internal Organisation

A mind is like a parachute
It doesn't work if it is not open.
Frank Zappa

Let's now move into the corporate world to take stock of changes that can be seen and felt in how business is conducted today. The developments that are taking place within companies are just as notable as those in the external environment.

Our world has become much smaller through being so inter-connected, but it is by no means homogeneous. Therefore, not all developments that I mention will concern every organisation in every geographical region. However, I have experienced first-hand that the changes I have chosen to highlight are becoming widespread across the globe.

We will now take a close look at four topics that I consider to be highly relevant to the role of leaders.

Changing dynamics within the workforce

Retirement ages are increasing, and as a consequence we are seeing an ageing workforce. At the other end of the employment spectrum, we have the Millennials. It is remarkable that today, companies may employ staff belonging to three or even four generation brackets. The oldest are likely to be found on supervisory boards. Different terms are used for different generations, but these are the most common:

- Traditionalists (born before 1945)
- Baby Boomers (born 1946–1964)
- Generation X (born 1965–1980)
- Millennials (born 1981–2001)

Each of these generations brings different experiences, beliefs, priorities and ambitions to the workplace. Each is characterised by different conduct, methods of communication and approaches in their daily work, but to many this colourful generational diversity feels frustrating.

The multigenerational workforce is a topic that has caught the eye of business psychologists, authors and consultants who share their wisdom on how to make it work in the interests of all concerned. The vast majority of books refer to a contentious gap between the generations, and there appears to be a general consensus that a deeper understanding of the generations will help to close the gap and bridge differences. However, if seeking to bridge gaps is the objective, we may see too much compromise, underused talent and a restriction of creativity.

I am in favour of generating a deeper understanding between

generations, but I would focus on building synergy thanks to and not despite their differences.

Intergenerational leadership is a vital skill that I believe will set executives apart from their peers who have not made this a priority of their leadership agenda. There is no point taking a neutral stance and expecting everyone – two, three or even four generations – to work side by side in complementary formats just because they are responsible adults and should know how to get along. That is a passive, reactive approach. What senior executives need is to provide guidance and foresight.

It takes a courageous leader to take down naturally formed barriers, rule out stereotyping, and define and demonstrate the unique value proposition of each generation. Blending adaptability and cross-functional learning into each of the generations will jump start a more dynamic knowledge-sharing culture. This is the type of internal variation that facilitates creativity and drives productivity. We will revisit this topic in Chapter Seven.

Another current topic in the corporate world is the position of talented and ambitious women. Sexism is widespread within companies, and macho-dominated business cultures tend to turn a blind eye to behaviour that feeds gender inequality. This is a surprising development in liberal Western societies. Extensive research by Utah State University researchers Alison Cook and Christy Glass and professors Michelle Ryan and Alex Haslam of the University of Exeter speaks of the prevalence of glass cliffs. Glass cliffs refer to the tendency to set women and minorities up to fail by handing them top roles that are highly risky and based on intractable tasks. The University of Exeter researchers analysed data from FTSE 100 companies and found that women are more likely to be appointed to top jobs in a crisis. These appointments usually follow a period of corporate underperformance or in critical situations when men have happily stepped aside. The UK's prime minister, Theresa May, is a good example of a woman coming on board and facing a cliff that may be steeper than any in its class.

Leading a company that faces immense risks cannot be compared to leadership in times of recovery or growth. The research also reveals that men usually win board positions at companies that are in an economically stronger state. Astounding statistics show that women and minorities in top positions are replaced by more traditional leaders when circumstances improve.

In a 2015 study published in *The Leadership Quarterly*, Utah researcher Alison Cook reported that fifty-two women CEOs were appointed to a Fortune 500 company in 2014. She found that 42% were appointed during times of crisis, versus just 22% of men CEOs. On the other hand, 70% of men CEOs were appointed when the firm was doing well, while only 44% of women CEOs took on the job when business was booming.

The closer they get to board functions, the more strategically and politically savvy women have to become. Recognising glass cliffs is part of a leader's required skillset. Seeing promotions for what they are in the context of both internal and external circumstances is crucial to making the right decision and creating the right framework to manage expectations.

My final point regarding prevalent internal dynamics concerns businesses' unquenchable thirst for quantifiable data. Management teams find much comfort in analysing spreadsheets and focusing on consolidation in times of uncertainty. Cost cutting is based on extensive profitability analysis. Top executives find a new area to focus on and send infinite requests for further analysis to department heads. Consolidation becomes the norm for many executives. In this process, the organisation becomes too inwardly focused and removed from the customer. Decisions based on data alone do not produce the best outcomes. The most creative ideas come from personal contact with business partners and a human understanding of their interests.

Flatter organisations and self-managed teams

The transition from hierarchical organisational structures to flatter structures is not new. The difference today is the speed and extent to which this change is happening. Reorganisations are taking place in favour of flatter management structures even in sectors traditionally known for their hierarchies and strict lines of communication.

For some organisations, this is a strategic choice to adjust to modern times in which greater employee participation is considered a prerequisite for an energised and high performing workforce. For other organisations, for example in the airline industry and banking, urgent financial considerations have driven the process of delayering. Whatever the motivation may be or may have been, these changes do not take place without considerable disruption. Some employees gain and others lose authority; spans of control are increased or functions become obsolete; peers become managers, supervising their former colleagues; double hatting, i.e. performing two roles, increases; people raise questions regarding fairness and the logic of decisions.

Once the hierarchical structure has been transformed to something less steep and the dust has settled, a different kind of challenge pops up. The greatest risk of all lies in leading a new organisational model in a traditional manner. Outdated systems of decision making, appraising staff and working within job descriptions are just a few examples of formerly accepted processes becoming horrible obstacles in a more dynamic environment. Less hierarchy requires that people are led differently, especially if the organisation has incorporated self-managed teams into its business model.

Flatter hierarchies have led to more transparency and shorter lines of communication. It is not surprising that these in turn have led to different forms of internal co-operation. Self-managed teams are on the rise. People fulfil multiple roles, and these may be on different teams.

Flatter organisations have also resulted in different points of contact between organisations and their customers. A big challenge companies face is how to increase access to customer related information from different pockets of the organisation. Speed and volume are recurring themes in a digitalised business world. Variation in types of customer related information and interaction has added to the challenge to extract maximum value from all channels of communication.

As departmental silos disappear, so do communication barriers. However, knowledge sharing has not come as naturally to employees as many companies would have hoped. Unfortunately, entering data and generating sales and forecast reports prevail over sharing and recording insights, experiences, and knowledge of customers' interests, including their business challenges and preferred styles of negotiation.

Not all leaders are skilled at leading change. Shortcomings in this area are more visible in flatter organisational structures than in highly hierarchical organisations. If management delays broad-based change initiatives, departments will set their own change agendas. Unfortunately, if their changes do not happen within the context of a broadly supported corporate direction, teams in different divisions will miss common ground when discussing improvements to work processes and closer co-operation. This will lead to fast and slow lanes in organisations, a 'we and they' mentality, and lots of dynamic activity that will not necessarily be effective or in the interest of the customer.

The impact of technology on the workplace

An increasing number of organisations allow employees to choose where they prepare their presentations, work on proposals, write reports or do research. All the technology available to staff has made them independent of a fixed workplace. Having a fixed desk in an office space may be becoming a thing of the past for many as hot-desking, working from home, and co-working hubs are becoming increasingly popular and accepted.

This is a trend that has developed faster than the mindsets of many company leaders. Some companies have chosen to give their employees ample trust and freedom. A BOYD (bring your own device) policy is becoming more common. This allows employees to use their own devices to access company information and applications. And then, at the other end of the spectrum, there are companies that use technology to monitor their employees' every move and maintain a system of full accountability. As can be expected, the companies that trust their employees gain positive PR on social media platforms.

As organisations adjust to this new form of work, they discover the need to have a more enticing central point to strengthen ties between colleagues. If loose ties and digital exchange of knowledge become the company's way of life, it generates a weakened culture and less engagement. This concern has led to the creation of headquarters that function as a modern hub with the best coffee in town, stylish areas to chat verbally with colleagues and share ideas, luxury work booths, trendy spaces for team sessions and all the top technology available to its workers.

Some multinationals have taken this luxury workspace to a whole new level. In his article 'Life and Workplace Health beyond the Office Cubicles' (FT *Health at Work*, September 2016), Edwin Heathcote sheds light on a different side of the seductively cool offices. Google's Tel Aviv offices have an artificial beach, and its London offices have beach huts. There are offices that turn into cocktail bars at 6pm, and yoga rooms and pool tables are part of the scene. At others, slides replace stairs after regular working hours to create a happy, playful work environment. Edwin Heathcote points out that ultimately the tech giants may intend to create not only a better work environment, but also a space where people stay for longer. Time will tell if staff will want to spend their free time in these environments. As Edwin Heathcote suggests, the healthiest workplace may be one you can leave easily to socialise with people other than your colleagues.

Whereas Google has emphasised playfulness and after work fun at its office buildings, Apple is set on offering its employees a more adult environment with workspaces and parklands to inspire them. Immaculate landscaping, including 7,000 trees and indigenous apricot orchards, surround Apple's new spaceship headquarters building in Cupertino. Bikes and electric golf carts help the staff to get around. The Apple HQ has been designed to give the 12,000 employees located there beauty in their surroundings during their working hours, but facilities are not available to encourage a 24/7 life at Apple Park.

This illustrates how different approaches regarding where and how employees spend their working time result in completely different environments. The purpose of any company's headquarters should be clearly defined. The priority should be thinking creatively about what to offer employees, freelancers, and even consultants or suppliers to encourage a strong feeling of connection to the company culture.

Technology has had a huge impact on how colleagues communicate with each other. This is where some generational differences surface. Baby Boomers prefer personal contact and will use the phone to set up a meeting. Gen Xers will send an e-mail, text or instant message and are happy to meet virtually. Millennials are connected at all times and send mainly instant messages or use a social networking site. The Millennials' messages and words are shorter, vowels are optional. To some employees, meeting a client means have coffee with a client; to others, it means connect online. To 'chat' may mean verbal contact to one and instant messaging to another.

Whatever the employee's preference, technology has on the one hand brought more excitement and pleasure to professions, and on the other has generated challenges. Dealing with these challenges is still a work in progress. E-mails have become a curse for many who have overflowing inboxes. E-mails are one-way messages, and too many are sent from someone in a passive reactive work mode. It is, therefore, not surprising to hear that companies are looking into real-time messaging platforms to replace e-mail.

Examples of messaging systems are Slack and Workplace by Facebook. These alternative messaging platforms prompt discussion, meaning the sender transmits messages in a proactive mindset. They support new team structures by facilitating discussion groups, sharing documents and using public and private channels.

At every workshop I lead, there are managers who mention the dilemma and frustration of attention-hijacking distractions. Some senior managers report that they spend only one-third of their time doing what they believe they ought to be doing. There is no easy solution to the overload of communication. Some people will overuse any chat option, and others will feel bogged down by the repetitive action of responding to messages from those who ask before thinking or comment incessantly. A policy that facilitates the most effective and balanced use of all messaging systems would, I am sure, be welcomed by employees across the board.

Technology is also transforming career advancement within organisations. IBM's Blue Matching programme is an example of a system that uses analytics to identify internal positions that match employees' experience, role, performance and location. Some organisations are also including employees' hobbies in their search data to capture all possible talents. This form of self-service career mobility diminishes the role of managers who formerly had a decisive say regarding the timing and nature of their direct reports' internal promotions. This technology could prove to accelerate employees' professional development.

Technology is also the context in which loneliness has crept into many societies, including the corporate world. Social media can enhance loneliness, as can working in a virtual office environment. Research shows that feeling lonely can even occur in office buildings where hundreds of colleagues work in close proximity to one another. Managers have a role to play to ensure that the benefits of technology do not come at the high price of employees feeling isolated and undervalued.

The challenges are clear. Where's the opportunity? Opportunity lies in using the best technology to increase efficiency and productivity while ensuring it supports personal interaction. Digital transmissions of information and knowledge are an asset, but the most effective way to gain leadership and business skills is to also have face-to-face interaction on the job.

The deadline-driven work mode

I am not even going to try to paint a balanced picture here. This is where I see only risks, and I base this section on years of experience working with vast numbers of senior managers of all nationalities.

The top levels of organisations are grappling with an over-load of information, overfull agendas, fast-moving changes, problems that demand immediate attention, and a good share of firefighting activities, too. Senior managers who have fallen into the trap of reacting quickly to all these trade valuable leadership time for a trouble-shooting man-agement style. Their reactive deadline-driven work mode is projected for all to see when they become slaves to their digital devices, and every ring, beep or vibration switches them from their conversation to checking the incoming message. The impression is that circumstances, not they, control their time.

This reminds me of a conference I led in Sofia some years ago. The participants, all holding senior positions, sat down and carefully positioned their mobile phones in prime posi-tions. To be called during a meeting was a sign of importance, and there was an interesting pattern in how frequently each phone rang. The participants did not appear embarrassed when their phones rang. I even got the impression some knew at what time their phones would ring.

By lunchtime on the second day, they realised they were missing too much course content with each call. After some diplomatic intervention from my side, we did not see another mobile phone until the end of the conference. As I was invited back to Bulgaria, they must have found peace during the conference without their phones and not an uncomfortable sense of abandonment.

Although top executives have, in general, retained their personal or executive assistants, less secretarial or admin-istrative support is allocated to managers across the board. Digital products have made it easier to execute a range of

THE CHANGING FACE OF THE INTERNAL ORGANISATION

processes, and these activities have slowly found their way to senior managers' desks. Designing PowerPoints, completing spreadsheets and dealing with an e-mail overload have, for many, become a part of the daily routine. Such activities claim too much valuable time at the expense of activities that allow leaders to make a real difference. This is an issue that requires attention and action.

Many senior managers admit to having a short-term focus and reactive work mode, and they tend to blame this on the phase of the company – anything from a departmental reorganisation to a period of extensive expansion. However, the reality is that stability is not going to return. As long as a high percentage of senior managers demonstrate they cannot let go, they are setting an example for less senior managers to lead in the same ad hoc manner. This could result in losing high-potential employees and making the company less adaptable and quick to respond.

It is impossible to lead by example from a position of keeping several balls in the air and missing what matters most. To move beyond this way of working, leaders need to redefine their roles and assess the required skillset to make a meaningful difference.

We will discuss this topic further in Chapter Four.

False assumptions

Let's now look at two assumptions that are still going strong in internal business environments. I consider the first assumption to be an excuse and the second to be a red flag.

Assumption 1: Giving employees maximum freedom leads to higher productivity.

It is widely believed that giving employees lots of freedom will increase their motivation and productivity. This is not necessarily the case.

Let's first look at two types of freedom.

To free staff from hurdles in business processes, bureaucratic procedures and other issues that hinder work pleasure and effective methods of co-operation is an important task for any leader. Being free from such matters gives employees a valuable sense of space and relief, until another obstacle occurs. Therefore, this freedom requires regular attention.

And then there is the freedom employees feel to do things. This is the freedom to make choices regarding an approach, a strategy or method of implementation to achieve the agreed objectives.

The first type of freedom is easier to arrange. Once a leader has discovered unwanted practical limitations, these can be partially or entirely removed. The second type of freedom is a more sustainable freedom, the intrinsically motivational kind, and I see time and again that it is more difficult for leaders to get right.

When leaders do not get the 'freedom to act' strategy right, they usually give others too much freedom. The result is likely to be a lack of productivity, and in the worst case even stagnation. This can be disappointing for executives who do not understand why employees don't value the freedom they've so generously given. But that freedom did not have boundaries providing clarity.

Examples of boundaries that leaders need to communicate are the extent of the authority given to individuals, a department or team; the direction of the company; the type of results that support that direction; the external developments to be taken into account; important strategic questions on the corporate agenda; or the company's international corporate policy. Without this framework there may be lots of activity, but not the level of productivity or the right kind of progress that increases profit. Individuals may waste time on hesitation and team disagreements. Added to this, there will be no trustworthy criteria to guide decision making and conflict resolution.

Therefore, the notion that maximum freedom is a good thing is usually wrong. If senior managers are in the reactive deadline-driven work mode, then they are either exerting too much control or giving too much 'freedom'. Authority and autonomy within agreed parameters is what gives real freedom and stimulates creativity. It asks leaders to put more time and effort into looking ahead, creating context, and involving employees in the big questions.

Assumption 2: Everyone on the same page – the recipe for business success.

'We're on the same page'; 'We're singing from the same hymn sheet' – such phrases are frequently used expressions in business to describe everyone being in agreement or supportive of a process, decision or strategy. The Dutch refer to 'all noses pointing in the same direction', the French say that people 'act in concert'. No one can disagree that operations run more smoothly if everyone is on the same page. The USA women's relay team would not have won gold in the 4×400 metres at the 2017 Athletics World Championships if they had all been running in different directions. And spectators cringe when synchronised divers end up not diving in synchronisation. So being on the same page is a good thing if we are referring to the execution of an activity or the end result.

But in all other phases of communication this is not a good thing. Frequent use of this or a related expression should be considered a red flag.

The problem in the Western business world today is that managers want quick results and strive to get everyone agreeing at an early stage. In process phases where nothing is more valuable than diverse ideas, there should be no emphasis on agreeing. This is the creative phase and it is here that people feel engaged and committed to finding the third alternative. It is in this phase that a company builds a competitive advantage.

Taking short cuts to generate or force agreement usually stems from a short-term focus, quick win objective or the desire to avoid conflict. There is nothing wrong with conflict, but it is the leader's role to guide it. When leaders speak of the need to be on the same page, this is usually done with the best of intentions. The paradox, however, is that chasing a quick agreement usually results in a long-term process for all concerned. A string of meetings follows to discuss disagreements, tackle underperformance or revisit the purpose and plans. Whether these are stand-ups or longer, traditional meetings, the outcome will usually be the same: the need to meet again.

If a process lacks dynamic energy, it is likely that too little value has been attached to differences or healthy debate.

This can alienate high potentials from a process in which their added value may otherwise have been priceless, which has contributed to initiatives, primarily among younger workers, to set up a team-driven structure of cross-functional co-operation.

Even though looking for similarities may come naturally to people, looking for differences will make everyone wiser and more energised. A well-led process of exploring differences is likely to result in cohesion and faster results.

Opportunities for leaders

It is time to reflect on what we could do differently to strengthen our influence as leaders and turn developments to the company's advantage. Again, we will look at diverse areas of focus that would add value to your agenda.

Responding to internal factors

AREA OF FOCUS	EXAMPLES OF STATEMENTS TO CONSIDER	✓/x
Profile of the workforce: generational and gender dynamics	• Your company has a policy or guidelines in place to create generational synergy • Gender dynamics are observed, discussed and given sufficient attention	
Flatter organisation	• Your senior colleagues and you have adapted your roles and leadership styles to the needs of an evolving business structure • You are aware of changing team dynamics	

AREA OF FOCUS	EXAMPLES OF STATEMENTS TO CONSIDER	✓/x
Technology at work	• Your company discusses how best to respond to the further use of digitalisation in work processes	
	• The policy of using HQ and satellite work spaces is consistent and supportive of the desired business culture	
	• Technology is consciously applied to strengthen valuable face-to-face interaction	
Ad hoc work mode	• You have taken time to observe whether this pattern is prevalent in your company	
	• There is an acceptance that restricting this work mode will lead to more effective leadership	
	• You are aware of what you could do differently to counteract this reactive task-driven leadership style	
Engagement and productivity	• You are satisfied with the level of trust and clarity given to employees to enhance initiative taking, knowledge sharing, optimal productivity	
Focus on differences or similarities	• The right procedures are in place to capitalise on differences	
	• You apply and encourage the use of questioning, listening and observation skills	

This table can be downloaded at http://www.jpcint.com/publications

Please use the blank cells to add any other area of focus based on your own business situation. Then put a tick or cross next to each statement to indicate if it is/is not applicable to you/your organisation.

Now select three areas you wish to prioritise, basing your choice on what you know now. It is not necessary at this stage to go into any form of internal analysis. By selecting these topics, you have chosen to do any of the following for each of them:

- Observe processes in practice to establish the current relevance and importance of this topic
- Introduce the topic for policy and strategic purposes
- Challenge others
- Promote this topic internally
- Study this topic further
- Translate it into a KSF
- Build a reputation in this field
- Demonstrate its importance by setting a clear example to others

Summary

This chapter was about gaining an understanding of significant developments that are evolving within organisations. Four developments we discussed are:

- Changing dynamics within the workforce
- Flatter organisations and self-management teams
- The impact of technology on the workplace
- The deadline-driven work mode

We also addressed two false assumptions and how these have a negative impact on productivity and progress. The assumptions we challenged are: 'Giving employees maximum freedom leads to higher productivity' and 'Everyone on the same page – the recipe for business success.'

We ended this chapter with an exercise to help you relate all you have read to your own business environment. Now you have selected areas you will focus on, the following chapters will help you to think of steps you could take to turn circumstances to your and your company's advantage.

What is the impact of external and internal forces on leaders, and what dilemmas do they present in a period of significant transition? These are the key questions we will address in the following chapter as we step into the reality of leadership today.

3

Leadership Today – the Transitional Phase of Half Measures

A peaceful world is good . . . but if it is always like that,
then nothing really improves.
Kazuo Inamori, Founder of Kyocera

This is where we will get a bit more personal and look into how leaders are coping in the turmoil of our world today. How are they responding to changing demands and dilemmas at home and abroad? Are leaders currently in a phase of transition as companies evolve? These are questions we will be answering in this section before we look at powerful alternatives.

Organisational transformations

There have been significant organisational transformations in recent decades. Some organisations have evolved slowly and adopted new processes as and when they needed them. Others have leaped forward and transformed their structures and business models to take the lead in demonstrating new ways of co-operation.

In our dealings with organisations today we will come across various organisational structures. Some we may consider outdated, and others so modern that they challenge us to step over a few biases. The nature of the organisation, the political and economic spheres in which it operates, and the sector in which it is active are factors that have a certain level of influence on how a company is run. I emphasise the word *certain* as our highly-connected digital world is challenging the supremacy of hard-core tradition.

I will highlight four different kinds of organisations in the order of when they came into being. We still see examples of all of them today.

Organisations anchored in hierarchy and control

Although hierarchical organisations started way before the 20th century, we need not go that far back in time to arrive in a world where hierarchical structures were the norm. Senior managers set the agenda, and control was a buzz word – control of processes, people and tasks. Subordinates were expected to carry out instructions in a disciplined and conscientious manner. People fulfilled certain roles and lines of communication were respected. Work was stable and predictable. Knowledge was power in the sense that knowledge was shared among the highest-ranking managers. Below them, information sharing was on a need-to-know basis and usually restricted to instructions. Authority and status went hand in hand with leadership positions.

In pyramid-style organisations employees are inclined to become loyal to their departments, serving their department's interests above the interests of the organisation as a whole. Therefore, there is always the risk of rivalry which, combined with the prevalence of bureaucracy, can impede change.

Close to home or further afield you will find organisations that fit into this mould. The military is an obvious example of where this way of working feels right and suitably accommodating of the required discipline and focus.

Organisations anchored in management by objectives

As industrial and technological developments increased the pace of business, the old top down structure could not be sustained in many sectors. Competition was increasing and internal potential was going to waste. Something had to change.

Effectiveness, efficiency, research and development, and shared responsibility became examples of new areas of focus. Business activities were modernised, including HR and marketing. Branding became paramount in a competitive environment, and along came KPIs and management by objectives in order to increase and sustain growth. In time, more freedom was given to employees in how they achieved certain targets, even though senior management still determined what those targets should be. Employees' career progress depended more and more on their talents and achievement.

As profits grew, managers focused more narrowly on increasing turnover and safeguarding margins for maximum profit. Objectives became shorter term, and the desire to win and gain more benefits was often not tamed. There are plenty of examples of unethical practices, both within organisations and in external environments, that were used to amass more wealth.

A narrow focus generally leads to many blind spots, often to the detriment of stakeholders.

Are organisations built on management by objectives still around today? Definitely. Take a look at the majority of multinationals. This is where you can detect the foundations of management by objectives, short-term focus, the emphasis on accountability, materialistic values and goals, and the existence of internal competition.

Is this sustainable? Yes, to a certain extent and at a price. This model can be tweaked to meet changing needs, but there is no doubt that a percentage of leaders and employees start at some point to seek a deeper meaning to what they do, or simply long for a sense of fulfilment. A steep increase in negative stress and burnouts has been recorded in this business model. Disengagement is a damaging development within any organisation, and talents move on to where they feel more at home.

Organisations anchored in empowerment

With employees and their leaders seeking a higher level of motivation within their organisations, KPI-driven processes were no longer wanted or considered effective.

Empowerment became a main driver in achieving higher levels of engagement and stimulation.

This type of organisation focuses on the benefits of co-operation, knowledge sharing and equal opportunities. The employee is considered a vital asset. Training and support are provided to strengthen employees' personal development and sense of belonging. Recruiters' selection criteria include soft management and interpersonal communication skills. Intercultural sensitivity becomes a must-have attribute for those seeking a global function.

Both small and large organisations have adopted this empowering style of co-operation. It is most likely to be fully incorporated in organisations that have integrated social responsibility into their business models. If companies have built their reputations on ethical standards and a positive impact on society, then they are likely to have a more informal atmosphere, team consultations and a higher level of flexibility.

Organisations anchored in empowerment have changed the face of leadership in many companies. Despite the position this more avant-garde business model has earned in the business community, for many it feels like unfinished business. Some companies have declared their employees 'empowered' without creating the required conditions that facilitate empowerment. Others have gone too far in pursuit of an egalitarian working environment resulting in time-consuming processes. A certain level of hierarchy is necessary to retain focus and pace through effective decision making.

Organisations anchored in self-management

For many employees who got a taste of increased responsibility and authority, and had at their disposal the means
to work more efficiently thanks to ground-breaking digital
solutions and promises, the empowerment model proved
to have its limitations. Spells of team-driven innovation felt
really good, and the demand grew for a better framework
to make this new way of working sustainable – a pillar of
the future organisation.

Employees wanted more autonomy, team synergy and influence, as well as a deeper sense of purpose. People developed
a dislike for traditional formats. For them, home and work,
personal qualities and professional skills, business objectives and personal ambitions, no longer belonged in six
different boxes, but needed to overlap for one complete
identity. I mentioned self-managed teams when we zoomed
in on current internal developments. Well, this is where they
belong: in this progressive organisational structure.

This kind of organisation does not happen naturally. It
takes excellent leadership and well-structured processes to
achieve effective self-management. When companies get it
right, I do not believe there is a more rewarding, engaging
or successful business model in our fast-paced environment.
Innovation will depend on it.

I have much more to share with you on this topic, as you
will see in the following chapters.

All of these organisational structures exist today. Some
organisations have adapted their business models, others
have taken more radical steps to instigate a completely

different and more mature system of co-operation. There is much a company can learn by doing, but targeted observation and good preparation can ensure the right framework is put into place to achieve effective self-management processes and the correct level of autonomy.

Self-management may suggest a leader is put on the back-burner. Or, they will be transformed into a ceremonial figure who showcases the latest innovations, team results and improvements in diversity. That is a misconception. It does not even come close to the indispensable added value that is required of a different kind of leader – the kind of leader who leads for tomorrow.

Leadership in transition – the risk of half measures

Given the pace of external and internal development, virtually all companies are in a phase of transition as they modernise processes to retain talent, facilitate innovation, and become more competitive. Transitioning from one organisational structure or business model to another demands much of leaders. If changes are incremental, leaders are able to adjust their styles in a step-by-step process. If circumstances demand a quicker, more influential response, then character, even more than skill, can help leaders to adapt with less hesitation. A willingness to accept other perspectives and discover new prospects, as well as the awareness of one's personal biases, can smooth the path towards making confident choices.

The current phase of organisational development, the organisation anchored in self-management, is one of the most exciting leaders have ever faced. It is also one that can be ruthless towards leaders who find themselves in a cycle of half measures. When developments outpace the evolution of the business model, the leader's performance is dictated by circumstances instead of forward thinking.

Problems arise when a leader has one leg in a traditional business model and the other leg in a more modern business model. While keeping some business processes the same, the leader implements exciting new changes, but only piecemeal to avoid disruption. Or, when they run into difficulties, they may resort to old practices. It is beyond half measures that real transitions – the professionally and economically rewarding kind – take place.

There are two types of half measures – the first concerns the leader's personal role and the second concerns the leader's business decisions.

Half measures in a personal context

The devil lies in authenticity

Leaders seeking to strengthen their identity and positioning will want to be seen to excel in certain areas and be known for prized attributes. This is a sensible and constructive means to get ahead. It is also the most effective way to manage a personal reputation. If, however, leaders speak mainly of their objective to remain authentic, this has to be examined a little more closely.

A desire for authenticity has been fuelled by consultancy companies and the media since the turn of the century.

Management teams have enrolled on authentic leadership courses in large numbers as they face an acceleration of disruptive external developments. No one could disagree with the importance of leaders staying true to their values and not crossing ethical boundaries, but how often are leaders asked to cheat, discriminate or destroy morale? If any of this were asked of you, I am sure your moral conscience would not allow it. Remaining authentic is generally not used in that context.

Studies show that when a leader calls on their authenticity, it does not refer so much to ethical questions as to a comforting justification for not stepping into areas that are unfamiliar or daunting. For example, if a chartered accountant were asked to be the company's ambassador at high-profile global conferences, he might reject this opportunity if he considered himself to be too introvert. By protecting his authenticity as an introvert he imposes unnecessary restrictions on himself.

Even the most senior leaders face the secret fear of vulnerability from time to time, and they may be subconsciously stopping themselves from learning from their subordinates in a field they are less familiar with. If they see themselves only as leaders, they won't want to lose status by being seen as a beginner. If their image of their authenticity is that they remain who they are, they are limiting who they could be.

If authentic leadership encourages you to lead based on who you have been until now, this doesn't imply progress. Which original version of yourself are you wishing to preserve? We all change and develop, and must continue to do so, especially in this world of disruption that demands a creative and courageous response from leaders. Therefore, consider the possibility that preservation of the current *you* may be holding you back from doing something challenging. It is in the brave area of trial and error that real development takes place and reputations are established.

Not every opportunity you are offered will be one worth taking. If a choice feels wrong, trust your judgement and do not make it. However, it is worth taking a step back and questioning the motivation for your decision. What is blocking you from full acceptance of an opportunity?

There is another area in which authenticity is being exploited. Authentic speech has taken on a whole new meaning in the age of populism. Here authenticity is used as an excuse to allow people to say anything in any manner. Emotion above facts.

After years of political correctness, we now hear populist politicians, particularly in the USA and across Europe, using so-called authentic speech to appeal to the fears and pre-judices of voters. The populists speak their minds without an intelligent filter to emphasise how citizens are being mistreated by the elite. Their almost exclusive use of heated emotion packed with scornful statements appeals to the target audience, who are pleased to have a furious, vociferous champion on their side. There is no self-censorship or sense of shared responsibility, but the speakers pride themselves on being authentic.

There are two sides to the authenticity coin. Only by using an intelligent filter does it remain a virtue.

Leaders act on the premise of 'more' instead of 'different'

When a company transitions through new phases, the positions of senior leaders change too. These phases may be cycles of turbulence, steep growth, a new strategy, fast business development, international expansion, a merger or consolidation. I have often experienced ambitious leaders committing to taking on a far larger scope of responsibility before thinking of which choices they need to make to be successful in their new roles.

This is where leaders enter a danger zone. All new challenges and dynamic forces are exciting, and as there is never any time to waste, some leaders are inclined to leap forward, tackle issues and make a stir. They dive into the content and roll out activities to increase the company's sense of urgency and their own impact.

What leaders tend to delay is defining their own professional framework. What will their role be? What will change in their new field of expertise? What will they be doing differently? What will they no longer be doing? Who needs to know? Which choices will be made regarding mutual expectations? Which skill or talent will they need most? Who will the new stakeholders be? Getting this right is as important as the task that lies ahead.

The consequence of the 'more' approach, e.g. more authority, more importance, more attention for internal or external influences, is that leaders end up either micromanaging or working against the clock, delivering everything in half measures, coping not excelling. Innovation stalls, teams become restless, potential is wasted, and employee disengagement lurks.

Have you ever wondered why time management still features in training programmes offered to middle and senior management? This almost archaic topic has survived all storms. In my opinion, this is because the results are not sustainable and this necessitates refresher courses.

Time will not be managed; it ticks on. Choices and use of energy, on the other hand, can be managed, and this has never been more important. Perpetually doing more in less time will exhaust you, or at least severely increase your coffee intake.

Leading for concrete change should not be on the premise of more. I believe in making choices for a different role, letting go in some areas and excelling in others. This will ensure leaders can perform their chosen priorities well, identify opportunities early on, build a reputation for certain qualities and enjoy a greater sense of inner and external influence.

New business models cannot survive successfully if the leader does not lead by example. As soon as you take on a new level or area of responsibility, put your energy into creating your new professional framework. This is not a one-off activity; it needs to be renewed whenever your focus and responsibilities change. It is a golden opportunity to make a fresh start and legitimately use the reset button.

Imagine how having a personal professional framework would help managers who are promoted to positions above their peers. If they had a plan based on their new role and relationship with their team, they would be able to prepare effectively and avoid much trial and error. A classic example of an ineffective approach in such situations is a newly promoted colleague seeking to gain support from their former peers by retaining the relationship they have always had. Simply adding responsibilities to an existing role will base the manager's new role on compromise.

Half measures in strategic business conduct

At this time of ongoing organisational development, there are two areas in which I have detected half measures in business conduct that can be costly, particularly if a leader is wanting to lead a change process.

Indecisiveness

Decisiveness at a strategic level is a must, not a 'nice to have' competency.

DECISIVENESS: A VITAL QUALITY

Some years ago, I worked closely with a CEO, Mr X. Mr X had been through a period in which he had attempted to improve the functioning of his marketing department. Because the company was considered to be one big, happy family, Mr X was cautious not to bring about change that would upset any of his 500 staff members, and he believed they would feel threatened if he were to engage an external party to carry out the project.

It so happened that there were two senior managers in his international sales department who were ready for a new challenge. Mr X selected them to work alongside the marketing department to create a proposal to make the department more agile, willing to liaise with colleagues, and able to tune into customers' needs effectively. To ensure the project managers would not exert authority, Mr X did not formally appoint them to their new roles, and they worked in a peer-friendly, low-key manner.

This undermined their credibility.

Many months later, Mr X approved version seven of the project managers' proposal and the time had arrived for implementation. Mr X chose to implement the changes that were safe and would put minds at rest. Step by step felt good to him.

However, the changes had no chance of succeeding without the proposed supporting framework in place. They were perceived by many to be symbolic, worthless and, in fact, destructive. This led to ridicule of the company's lack of resolution, pace and adaptability. Mr X's reputation as CEO suffered a blow.

In retrospect, Mr X realised he had applied the wrong approach. The core issue had been that he'd agreed it was time to change, as long as most of the changes fitted neatly into the 'business as usual' framework. Micromanaging and reluctant decision making were his recurring pitfalls.

So how can one avoid ineffective decision making, and what is the cause of these counterproductive measures? Let me first tell you the main reasons leaders have mentioned to me for being poor strategic decision makers.

Common examples of poor decision making

REASONS GIVEN FOR A PATTERN OF POOR DECISION MAKING	HOW VALID IS EACH REASON? MY RESPONSE
I made a few errors of judgement due to incomplete information	Errors of judgement are not the real issue. They are part of the game. It is more likely that the process of collecting the right information is flawed
I have been too busy	Being too busy is an excuse that is often used to camouflage poor priority setting

REASONS GIVEN FOR A PATTERN OF POOR DECISION MAKING	HOW VALID IS EACH REASON? MY RESPONSE
My lack of technical knowledge	This can lead to insecurity, but should not disqualify a leader's ability to make a sensible decision
I tried to keep the troops happy	Not a wise basis on which to make an important decision. However, a proper decision-making process is probably lacking
Can't trust key people to give me objective information	Bad news, but not likely to be the driver behind poor strategy and decision making
Cultural clashes within the organisation	Problematic indeed, but remember that a weak culture needs effective strategic decision making. Who is waiting for whom?
Lonely at the top	A tough place to be for any leader, but not a good excuse for poor decision making. It is more likely that a framework for effective knowledge sharing is missing
Too many regulations	Difficult to contend with, but do regulations drive decision-making processes? Even more reason to take ownership of the big issues and address limitations
Opposing points of view within the management team	This can end up in unfortunate compromise. However, different opinions, if channelled well, lead to a better outcome, not a poor decision

As my responses reveal, these reasons are excuses or obstacles, and not the cause of poor decision making.

During many years of working with leaders, I have discovered that the more disruptive the environment, the more likely we are to observe a pattern of indecisiveness, and therefore poor decision making. The key to the problem is what I call the false security of half measures, which leads to poor decision-making processes.

How can leaders turn this around in a world of increasing complexity? The answer lies in one simple word: CONTEXT

Defining the context

To define the context is to describe a situation with complete clarity and attach a purpose to it. The context describes important elements concerning an issue, such as the relevant circumstances, the desired outcome, the benefits, opportunities or risks. It gives meaning to the situation or problem and helps you and others to visualise it and put it into perspective. This is the foundation for any good decision making. Only when the context makes sense and is communicated to others in a meaningful way will leaders make the right decisions.

Once the context is clear, minds can focus on discussing the matter with a view to creating better results. Without a clearly defined context, leaders cannot explain situations clearly and will base decisions on narrow problem solving.

The most influential leaders never enter a negotiation, a gathering with the work council, or a meeting with suppliers without first thinking of the purpose of the meeting, the relevant circumstances, the opportunities and risks. The context gives them the confidence to communicate and manoeuvre successfully in different settings.

If a manager chooses piecemeal implementation of something new, they are probably too focused on action points. Another example is how a leader delegates. If they delegate tasks rather than responsibilities and authority, the leader has probably not taken the time to put the project into any kind of context. The short-term to-do-list is their key focal point. Therefore, they delegate tasks, and the project as a whole leads to disappointing results.

Agreeing on the context builds synergy and unites people, whereas decisions and leadership styles that are task driven have a way of causing conflict. Creating compelling contexts is the most enjoyable side of business at a senior level today. Leaders do not need to be the most visionary people; listening to people who provide relevant data and knowledge is the stepping stone to creating a context people will buy into. Leaders require this skill more than ever before as a higher percentage of the workforce does not want to be led by delegation of tasks, but by involvement in the purpose of the project or organisation.

How do we know if the context is missing when we're making decisions? We simply look to see if the decision can or cannot be explained in the context of future progress.

Let me give you two examples.

Example 1: The context of diversity. A wide range of companies have a natural increase in diversity due to different generations in the workforce. Others have made an effort to become more diverse by employing more nationalities and people from a range of professional backgrounds. Gender diversity is central to most diversity programmes. And then there are organisations that maintain a culture of uniformity and homogeneity.

Why do some organisations excel in the field of diversity and others fail to make any concrete progress? For the answer, we need to look at the context in which diversity is addressed.

It is not uncommon to see that hitting certain diversity targets is considered evidence that companies are giving diversity the attention it deserves. However, the purpose of increasing diversity is often missing. For those companies, meeting targets is the end objective, not improving the business' climate or results. In such cases, there is no benefit in diversity. If the company policy makers are not able to sell the importance of these efforts beyond the argument that it is the socially correct thing to do, then there simply is no context that will generate broad support.

It is not time-consuming to develop a compelling context for diversity, which will improve the quality of debate and engagement between colleagues across the board. Thinking, speaking and leading in context has little to do with time and everything to do with forward-thinking leadership.

Example 2: The context of the modern workplace. Let's look at the modern workplace and the flexibility given to workers to choose their work location and methods they use to interact with their colleagues. Companies have had some years to adapt to this trend, so we may presume that they have developed a system of planning and organising that supports the new way of working. The question to ask ourselves is, 'How effective is that system?'

How can we tell if the system of working from home is part of a clear context? Look for clues to see if the flexible workplace policy is a narrow objective, or if it is an effective method to achieve a better work environment. If it is the narrow objective, companies will probably have implemented more control mechanisms to compensate for the flexible working arrangements granted to employees. Although the office has hot desks and trendy meeting areas, the company continues to reward traditional behaviour. The culture does not benefit from modern methods that build and strengthen co-worker ties in a flexible working format. You may even detect the same internal organisational silos, staff retaining the same desk at all times and unchanged work patterns.

As this behaviour demonstrates, switching to a flexible workplace was either a trade-off to satisfy employees or, equally limiting, it may have been based on a strategy to keep up with trends adopted by high-ranking employers. If this was the case, the driver of change was window dressing and not a new way of working to accommodate developments and opportunities. There was no definition of the purpose, benefits, boundaries and supporting procedures.

Policies and processes can only be implemented purposefully if there is a compelling context to support them.

Recruitment of talent – a shift to broader diversity

Recruiting the right people and providing the right environment for talent is a critical part of any business strategy. This is typically acknowledged in business plans used for both internal and external purposes. Yet, in most cases, what happens in practice is in stark contrast to companies adapting their hiring processes when seeking a different kind of talent. This is another area in which I have discovered the prevalence of half measures.

Most organisations use standardised systems for IQ, competency, behaviour, personality or technical ability testing.

The tests become an integral part of recruitment processes and are used for relatively long periods of time. Therefore, the same method of assessing talent is applied regardless of the kind of employee the organisation is seeking. Recruiters still gravitate towards candidates who are likely to fit in. They will be seeking the new skills and competencies the company is calling for, while also wanting to safeguard a culture of conformity.

Added to this, there is much evidence that people value characteristics in others that they recognise in themselves. Therefore, those candidates who interview along regular lines are more likely to be selected above those who may have exceptional intellectual abilities, but display characteristics that do not fall into familiar behavioural patterns.

As Professors Robert D. Austin and Gary P. Pisano highlight in their 2017 *Harvard Business Review* article 'Neurodiversity is a Competitive Advantage', many people with neurological disorders, including autism, ADHD and dyslexia, have extraordinary skills in pattern recognition, memory or mathematics. However, their research reveals that neurodiverse people suffer high unemployment – as high as 80%.

Professors Austin and Pisano explain how prominent organisations are developing programmes that will help to attract neurodiverse talent and provide the right environment and management for them. They give the compelling example of how the Israeli Defence Forces have employed a team of people primarily on the autism spectrum for their Special Intelligence Unit 9900. Their exceptional perceptual skills allow them to spot patterns others cannot see.

Early results show that neurodiverse environments lead to productivity gains, quality improvement and better innovation. Companies that reach out to neurodiverse people for areas in which specific intelligence is required, such as cybersecurity, engineering physics and data analytics are likely to achieve a considerable competitive advantage. However, they will need to provide suitable working conditions, for example quiet office spaces, and connect with expert support organisations to ensure neurodiversity works for all concerned.

Mediocre results will prevail if companies only semi-adjust the recruitment method to find employees with extraordinary talents. Artificial intelligence could offer a more objective preselection process if the predetermined selection criteria are changed sufficiently to target the right people. Therefore, to bring the best talent on board, we need a far broader view of the meaning of talent. Secondly, we must choose an approach that will not deliver ordinary, predictable outcomes. After all, there are more creative and effective ways than traditional interviewing methods to assess candidates' skills and potential.

Questions for leaders

I suggest we end this chapter with six leadership awareness questions. Please answer each question with Yes or No. I would then like you to then circle your No answers, as these will be your personal questions to carry over to the next chapters.

Leadership awareness

	LEADERSHIP AWARENESS QUESTIONS	YES OR NO
1	Is your company's business structure or business model in a phase of transition?	
2	Is it clear to you what the transformed business model or internal restructuring will look like a year from now, and how it will change employee working methods?	
3	Are you satisfied that your current organisational structure is suited to your company's objectives and internal and external developments?	
4	Would you say that the context of planned changes is as clear to those involved as the changes themselves?	
5	Have you consciously created your own professional framework?	
6	Have you reached the point that you can let go more and focus on new areas of importance?	

This table can be downloaded at http://www.jpcint.com/publications

Summary

Although organisational structures have changed considerably in the past decades, examples of both traditional and modern structures are present across sectors and regions. Some companies are modifying their structures, others are transforming them. We looked at the risk of applying half measures in this phase of transition and addressed half measures in personal and strategic business conduct.

Common causes of mediocre performance in a personal context:

- Using authenticity as an escape
- Failing to set the right priorities when taking on a higher level of responsibly
- Acting on the premise of 'more' instead of 'different'

Common causes of mediocre performance in business conduct:

- Indecisiveness
- Neglecting to create a compelling context
- Recruiting talent using outdated methods

We looked at the consequences of being hesitant in a disruptive environment and the most common reasons people give for poor strategic choices. These reasons are not the root cause of those poor decisions.

Defining the context of any dilemma or complexity is the first and most effective step towards productive debate and facilitated decision making. A context that is anchored in purpose provides focus and simplifies the questions at hand. Think about the value of creating contexts and practise using them to build support and increase your influence.

Finally, I asked six questions. By answering them, you will highlight areas to focus on going forward.

We are now ready to move on to how one prepares to be a different kind of leader.

4

Preparing for Change

I do not believe you can do today's job
with yesterday's methods
and be in business tomorrow.
Nelson Jackson

In this chapter we will deal with concrete steps to prepare for the demands of leadership today. Preparation is critical to any change in conduct or positioning. We will look at areas in which leaders can add considerable value to the organisation and to themselves.

Leaders

Let me clarify my use of the word leader. I refer mostly to business leaders and do so in the broadest sense of the word. However, the basic principles that apply to becoming a more influential business leader and responding effectively to current day challenges are applicable to leaders in all fields. All operate in the same world and face similar issues, regardless of their products, services and objectives.

To illustrate this, here are four examples of how diverse leadership roles beyond the corporate world are changing.

We will start with ambassadors. In 2015, diplomatic correspondent Bridget Kendall chaired an event on the changing world of diplomacy. The key speakers were Tom Fletcher, British Ambassador to Lebanon, and Sir William Patey, former British Ambassador to Afghanistan, Saudi Arabia and Iraq. Sir William Patey gave an insightful view on how the role of ambassadors is changing in a world where technology has made diplomacy much more public through blogging and tweeting. Embassies, too, face competition as risk consultancy agencies and other organisations offer analytical reports on countries and regions. The speed of news media means that the Foreign Office will first hear about an event overseas not from the embassy, but from the media. Therefore, there is now a greater need for ambassadors to use their analytical capabilities to deliver in-depth knowledge and analysis after the incident.

Tom Fletcher highlighted the importance of connecting with networks that are an unstructured moving power base. He referred to scientists' viewpoint that the change we will see in the next century is equivalent in sociological terms to the change in the last forty-three centuries.

Both speakers highlighted how diplomats will be transforming the way they work to retain an influential role in a world of robotics and big data.

The role of mayors is changing at an equally fast pace in our horizontally structured societies. If I limit this example to changes in Europe, we see that as people become disillusioned with their governments, they attach more value to the impartial role and craftsmanship of mayors. Meanwhile, mayors are increasingly vulnerable to critical media jeopardising their reputations and putting them on a slippery slope. Reputation management becomes more important at a time when mayors can no longer take their authority for granted.

The power of networks and technology are challenging mayors to work and lead differently. In societies that have become harsher and more individualistic, mayors must be quick to analyse information and enter into dialogue with different groups. They must be streetwise as they deal with issues ranging from an influx of refugees to security threats and incidents. Combatting jihadism and discrimination and offering protection for and from citizens with mental health problems is an ongoing concern.

From mayors to health care leaders. Watson Health, IBM's ground-breaking computer system, is influencing the role of leaders in the medical world. It can process millions of articles of medical data to provide an accurate diagnosis and treatment options within seconds. According to IBM's CEO, Ginni Rometty, the goal of the cloud-based cognitive computing system is to support doctors to make better diagnoses, not to replace doctors. With partners in different medical fields providing data, Watson is being trained to provide valuable diagnoses for ever more medical conditions. These partners help to create functional platforms available to doctors and specialists around the world.

What does this mean from a leadership perspective? Healthcare leaders work in an increasingly complex environment which puts a greater premium on their resilience and ability to drive innovation. Being externally focused and building partnerships are essential requirements. Medical partners now include IT experts, for example 3D printing specialists. Scans are turned into a 3D model helping surgeons to plan their approach in meticulous detail before performing an operation. For example, using 3D technology has been immensely helpful in the complex procedure of separating twins joined at the brain.

There is a fast-growing importance for leaders in the medical world to demonstrate the ethical use of advanced technology and engage in debates concerning new social and moral challenges.

My fourth example takes us into the emerging world of FashionTech. Designers who break through in this highly competitive market in the future will possess both digital and design skills, including coding. They will build their organisations by engaging staff members who excel in the use of digital technology and are also talented in the field of fashion design and artistry. Leadership will take on a whole new meaning for the design icons of the future.

Leading hi-tech fashion designer and innovator, Anouk Wipprecht, has made her name on the global stage with her tech-enhanced designs, bringing together fashion and technology: technological couture. Her robotic outfits move, breath and interact with the surroundings. Sensors in the design monitor the space around the wearer and body sensors check in on stress levels. Anouk Wipprecht continues to research new ways for our wardrobe to interface with the world around us.

I have summarised the changes that apply to leaders in four different sectors. Notice how all points apply to the corporate world too:

- All roles have increased in complexity
- There is a greater need for analytical, critical thinking
- Influence must be built where job- or skill-related authority was once a given
- More transparency and public engagement call for the intelligent use of data and media platforms
- There is a shift to leading for innovation
- An understanding of advanced technology is indispensable
- There is an even greater need for leaders in different sectors to demonstrate high moral values

These changes call for a different way of thinking. Design thinking is becoming an indispensable skill in disruptive environments where engagement and support cannot be achieved by cutting corners to solve problems quickly. Complexity calls for innovative outcomes.

Design thinking moves leaders away from spreadsheet-driven answers and problem solving. Using prototypes, models, drawings, diagrams and other objects to imagine what outcomes could look like helps leaders to explore innovative options and encourages others to share ideas. Defining challenges creatively and designing a path to new outcomes is as important as designing products and services. Those who are proficient in creating contexts are well on their way to developing the key competency of design thinking.

On the eve of self-management

As we demonstrated in the previous chapter, the most advanced organisational structure is anchored in self-management teams. We are still on the eve of the big sweep towards this organisational model. However, the majority of organisations are aware of this business structure and are considering implementing it, changing processes to accommodate it, or have joined the ranks of leading companies which have already embraced it. More on this topic later on.

Whatever your point of departure or objective may be, the approach, skills and thoughts I am sharing are intended for you. We don't lead for today or yesterday, but for tomorrow, and there is no doubt that you will at some point face the need to disrupt your own business. With competition increasing and technology racing ahead, it is better we disrupt ourselves than have another organisation do it to us. Former HP CEO, Lewis Platt, said back in the 1990s that in order to retain its leading position in printers, HP had to make its own products that were still selling well, obsolete and replace them with more advanced products.

This has never been more relevant than it is today. Given the pace of current developments, disruption should apply not only to products and services but also to business models and organisational structures. Disrupt or be disrupted.

As a different kind of leader, you will lead for advancement and disruption of the status quo, and at the same time enhance the engagement of employees and other stakeholders. We are now going to discuss three areas in which you can prepare for the new world of effective leadership.

Building awareness in each of these areas will put you in a stronger starting position.

Professional identity – think purpose

This is where you will create a professional framework. Even if you are the CEO of a large corporation and have received positive approval reviews in your current position, the only way to retain support and keep your organisation evolving is to reassess your own role from time to time. This is when you will discover new terrain requiring your involvement, activities that have become routine, or areas in which you have claimed too much ownership.

Most leaders have a written profile, or even a couple of versions of their profile for different uses. These may be on social media platforms, blogs, in newsletters or CVs. It is becoming customary for CVs and résumés to start with a personal profile. The kind of profile I am referring to is a compilation of adjectives that describes a person's background, main achievements, skills or competencies, and ambition. In highly competitive environments, people pay much attention to keeping their profiles current, building a strong identity, having a good elevator pitch and creating a positioning statement. All of this serves a valid purpose and that is to stand out from the crowd.

These written profiles are usually based on the here and now, listing a person's attributes in clichéd phrases. I believe this is too restrictive for leaders today. To drive change and deal successfully with a faster pace and more complexity, leaders need to be crystal clear about their purpose and what they stand for. To gain influence and lead for innovation, do not base your image on 'what is' or 'what has been' but on your path to 'what will be'.

I recommend you determine your leadership purpose as a starting point and not your unique selling points. This approach will help you to visualise yourself as a leader moving towards a certain goal. You will also become more in tune with how others are likely to see you in different settings. Establishing your professional purpose enables you to think beyond selling your qualities, making your added value and role visible, beneficial and almost tangible to others.

Let me take you through the creative and practical process in which you are going to craft your role.

Role

First, a short introduction. When I ask leaders about their professional roles, I find it fascinating to hear their different responses. The replies are often indicative of how they perceive their circumstances and level of influence.

I regularly hear a to-do list, complemented by responsibilities. It is so action orientated that all I remember is the volume of work and the heavy burden on the executive. This in turn creates a task-driven, hands-on image. I hope they can cope.

Sometimes a senior executive will speak primarily of their authority in different areas. In such cases the role sounds more interesting than the executive filling it.

Quite recently, during one of my workshops, an executive said his role was the same as that of the participant who had just introduced himself as they were both CFOs in the same sector. I do not believe any two roles are ever the same, and if they are, then more value is usually attached to an outdated job description than to the unique value of the executive. Given the complexity of a CFO's position, it can be tempting for a CFO to list their areas of responsibility. That, however, detracts from their influence. Each CFO needs to see their role and added value differently.

An effective role is a dynamic process leading to a destination. A role based on a purpose transforms a leader into a charismatic person worth following.

Picture the impact the CFO who said he had the same role as someone else could have made. Imagine if he had emphasised his key role as strategist to help influence the future direction of the company and mentioned his main areas of focus to achieve this: providing sharp financial analysis, facilitating expansion into the BRICS (Brazil, India, China and South Africa) countries, and transforming processes such as procurement to become more competitive on a global scale. I would want his business card, wouldn't you?

I have found that managers who move from being responsible for specialist work with measurable outcomes to global roles or positions of organisational or divisional management find it difficult to define their focus and added value. Where they formerly judged their success by the application of their in-depth knowledge, in the new situation, they will require different criteria. By defining the purpose of what we do, we transform how we position ourselves. We can then feel more excited about what we do because being on a mission gives a destination and soul to any professional function.

Ask yourself, 'If I excel in my position, what will this lead to?' The answer to that question is the purpose of your role. Make sure that it is challenging enough, and that the destination really is your destination and not an attractive stop on the way.

Take a look at the following example.

If you were a successful global commercial director, you could say that the purpose of your role is to achieve a dynamic sales force and satisfied clients. However, if you extend your horizon by answering a follow-on question, 'What would that lead to?', you would focus on *the benefits* of having a dynamic sales force and satisfied clients. A more accurate description of your role as global commercial director may then be 'to expand into new markets by focusing on developing a strong international sales force and building a larger and loyal customer base'.

Getting the role right will change your focus, your way of leading, your speech and your image. If your destination is happy customers, you will focus on pleasing them and your approach may be narrow, unilateral, reactive or predictable. If, however, international expansion is your destination, you will likely think of involving your customers in your innovation and services strategy to strengthen your market position and penetrate new marketplaces. You will speak differently, behave differently, use different criteria for decision making, and your distinctive style will allow you to lead by example.

Exercise: Create your role on a flipchart

This is an exercise to help you to get a sense of the purpose of your role and opportunities to increase your influence.

Draw a circle in the middle of the flipchart and put yourself at the centre of the circle. Add words that reflect your main responsibilities.

Now move out of the circle and jot down internal circumstances that you consider relevant to you in your position. Refer back to the final exercise in Chapter Two to see the three developments you earmarked as being most relevant to you, and add this shortlist here. Draw a circle around the internal developments.

Draw an outer circle encompassing the two inner circles. This is where you add the external developments that you highlighted at the end of Chapter One.

Mapping your Role

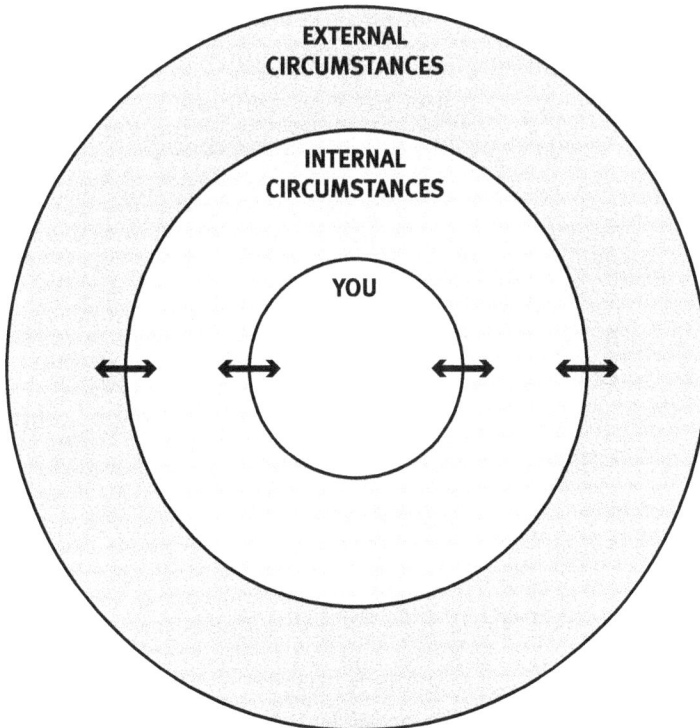

Reflect on the three circles. Flip over to a blank sheet. Think of what you would like to do with those internal and external developments and write your thoughts down. What could you do to make a bigger difference? Examples may be modernise specific processes, use technology differently (describe how), and increase team knowledge sharing to strengthen the organisation's competitive advantage.

Mapping your role. Use your notes to formulate the purpose of your role and what you will focus on to achieve that purpose. Add to this what your added value will be, and the experience or skills you will use to make things happen. You should not need more than four or five sentences.

Added value. If we were to rewind a couple of years, we would regularly run into the term 'personal branding'. Well, I am not about to suggest you develop a personal brand. It is too static and has a ring of permanence to it, like a tattoo. Remember, we are not going to remain authentic to what we used to be, so we are not going to brand ourselves. We are going to evolve in accordance with changing times and requirements, and as we progress, we want to be known for our added value.

Prepare to be known for three valuable qualities, and then turn these into credible, marketable assets. Be sure to stay clear of clichés. You achieve this by turning your qualities into an added value that is uniquely yours. Once you have chosen your qualities, build and manage your reputation around them.

Let me guide you through this process:

Choose the qualities you feel most excited about, ones you believe you will need in order to fulfil your role as a leader going forward. List them on a separate sheet, then follow the pattern of adding a destination. What is the purpose of your quality? In other words, what does it mean in practice?

Let's take the quality 'cultural sensitivity' as an example. What does it actually mean? Even if you are quick to sense cultural differences, 'sensitivity' does not imply you know what to do with them. And in the worst case, it may mean you get an allergic reaction to too much cultural complexity. Therefore, improve on how you describe this quality. Give it content and a purpose.

This is one of many ways in which you could reword your added value to reflect your real asset: 'I use my extensive understanding of multiple cultures to develop strong local leadership and employee engagement in different countries'.

Maybe you wrote that you are a skilled negotiator. That may mean you are a tough sales person, a terrier who does not let go, a kind person who methodically negotiates for an eventual 'win-almost win', or you negotiate from a position of power to cut suppliers' fees. Again, turn the quality into a differential advantage. Do you excel in negotiating based on mutual interests to grow your company's portfolio of international partnerships? If so, that's a pretty marketable asset to have, and it means a whole lot more than 'skilled negotiator'.

Take a few hours out of your busy schedule to work on this exercise. The result will be a role with a clear purpose, supported by your added value. It will provide a framework for sound decision making that will put you in a position of greater influence. Used well, that influence will be more sustainable and valuable than any formal authority.

Be consistent, not predictable

You now have a clear role, modified to be more in tune with your next twelve months as a leader, and it is supported by your unique qualities and focus. This brings us to the second topic that is indispensable as you prepare for change in how you lead. It is time to respond to the growing importance that is attached to consistency. Consistency breeds trust, and it should not be confused with predictability.

Predictability was acceptable for leaders in times of stability. I consider this a high-risk factor for leaders today. Consider this dictionary definition of predictability: *'Consistent repetition of a state, course of action, behaviour, or the like, making it possible to know in advance what to expect'*. We do not want to offer this level of comfort or boredom to our direct reports. Predictability can make us attached to patterns, a fixed routine, the same mannerisms and responses. I have observed how predictability can change a person's image and energy levels. Above all, it invites complacency.

Being consistent is a totally different ball game. Let's consider the ways in which consistency is described in different dictionaries: 'Harmonious uniformity among things or parts'; 'Being in conformity with guidelines, policies and values'; 'Harmony of conduct or practice with profession'; 'Logical coherence and accordance with the facts'. The words related to consistency, such as compatibility, coherence, harmony, correspondence and accordance, feel totally right for a leader in our times.

In order to demonstrate the value of consistency, we are now going to study where this is most noticeable: in how you communicate and in the choices you make.

Choice of words

Let's look at examples of inconsistencies to get a sense of the impact of ineffective communication. The best place to start is where we hear lots of business jargon. So, basically, everywhere.

Business jargon can be highly ineffective. Unfortunately it is also highly contagious. Many words are overused, and they either confuse the listener or fail to generate the kind of response the speaker expected.

In the era of management by objectives, many management terms were used that compared business processes to factory processes. These terms do not apply to current day developments. Certain words can suggest leaders are inconsistent if, for example, their words contradict their commitment. If they want to stimulate self-management across the board or facilitate innovation, but use words that belong to an older and more traditional management structure, then those words will undermine their messages and conduct.

Look at the following examples to understand how the use of management jargon can diminish a person's influence.

Input. We hear this word a great deal. Asking for input will usually lead to disappointment as the response will be minimal. Are you asking for additional details, general comments, a thorough review, a different perspective, confirmation that a document has been read, or seeking approval? The listener, not knowing what is expected of them, will deliver the safest of options, and it will be mediocre at best.

Unfortunately, in most cases the speaker doesn't really know what they are asking for. Using the word 'input' saves them thinking time, but it burdens the listener.

Output. If you state that the output should be improved, are you referring to the quality, quantity, efficiency, the chosen approach or the bottom-line results? The listener will use your vague words to question the value of your judgement. If, on the other hand, you question specific aspects of a project or performance, it is more likely that you will be appreciated for your keen interest and smart insights.

Feedback. Asking someone if they would like your feedback, or if they could give you their feedback, can be interpreted in multiple ways. What does feedback mean to you? Would you like to discuss the results of a programme, share ideas on new features or opportunities, talk about a declining market share or how a project can be extended to a new region? Be more specific to demonstrate your forward-thinking approach.

Address a problem. If you agreed to address two external risks, what did you have in mind when you made that statement? Does address mean that you will raise the risks at the next board meeting? Will you delegate them to someone for a thorough analysis and recommendation? Will you make them a top priority when you meet with your CFO? Or do you intend to make a decision this month based on the risk analyses already given to you? A concretely worded intention will increase your credibility.

Best practices. This is a particularly hollow term and one I hear far too often. It obviously sounds good to those who use it, but what do they mean?

In general, it suggests that they cut corners and use solutions or ideas that other companies have used in similar situations. However, no two situations are the same, and each company has its own context and circumstances. Best practices that do not originate from within the company can lead to resistance.

Given the pace of change in our environment, a best practice today should not be your blueprint for tomorrow. It is a good idea to learn from what others did well, but never use this term to bypass the steps that lead to real progress.

Take it to the next level. Picture an executive chairing an IT team meeting where the main agenda point concerns the successful launch of three new interlinked IT features. The executive is really happy. The team has worked gruelling hours to deal with much complexity, tight deadlines and a couple of setbacks. The results are way above expectation, as is the sense of satisfaction for everyone at the meeting.

Then the meeting ends on the executive's request to each team member to take this project to the next level. The IT team leaves, holding onto the positive vibes of the meeting and then puzzles over 'the next level'. 'What planet is he on?' they wonder. 'Which level? What needs to be improved? Go global? Create more of the same? Improve what we have just launched?' With no further ado, they decide to stick to their original plan and ignore what they consider to be the executive's nonsensical closing remark.

Had the executive given more critical thought to his expectations and been more explicit, the team may have felt encouraged by his remarks and not confused by them.

Actionable efforts. This belongs in the category of 'sounds good, but no idea what I am actually asking for'. If the CEO sends out a message asking the staff to make actionable efforts to increase productivity in the summer months, how many would understand the request or take it seriously? What is the difference between making an effort to increase productivity and making an actionable effort to increase productivity? By the time the recipients of the memo have worked it out, the summer may have come and gone.

Integrity and honesty. Although these are two of the most used core values on the websites of the world's largest corporations, in practice they invite scepticism. They have become clichés that do not give any insight into the corporate culture.

The more frequently these self-proclaimed virtues are used in an organisation, the more concerned I become. Rather than promote one's honesty, it is more effective to mention the conduct that supports it. This could be that mistakes are admitted openly.

Numerous companies have been exposed in recent years for public deceit, despite professing to have corporate values that often included the word integrity or honesty. Beware of the smoke screen.

Thinking outside the box. This overused cliché says more about the person who uses it than the listener. Which box?

In our current fast-paced world, we cannot afford to see boxes. Most Millennials certainly don't believe they are in one. When you ask others to think outside the box you are confirming the presence of one. As a leader in our environment today you cannot afford to accept that your organisation is in a box; one that should be left from time to time for innovative thinking. You need to remain out of all boxes and if you believe you or your team are in one, it is time to get rid of it.

People who refer to out-of-the-box see the box...
People who don't know the box even
exists are the innovative thinkers.
Lisa Goldenberg

The reactive out-of-office reply. 'I will be out of the office between date X and date Y and will not have access to my e-mails in this period'. Credible? No.

Using the technology excuse doesn't work these days. You would literally have to be on a remote island to have no access to any network throughout the period of your absence. And why the excuse in the first place? This could be inconsistent with the self-confidence you normally project.

A reply more consistent with a purpose-driven leadership style would be that you will not be accessing your e-mails in that period.

Never change a winning team. Many organisations develop routines for their activities and use repetition to become better at what they already do. They can become attached to existing, successful patterns. Leaders who use the phrase 'never change a winning team' undermine their credibility as leaders. How can they on the one hand want to promote an agile and resilient organisation built on the premise of ongoing advancement, yet on the other be reinforcing stability and routine?

These are just some examples of lazy business jargon that can undermine a leader's credibility. As complexity increases, there is an even greater need for executives to be specific regarding their expectations and decisions. Clarity of speech will enhance others' trust in you and increase your self-awareness of the impression you make. You will receive more immediate and open responses and better dialogue. I encourage leaders not only to reduce their use of vague terms, but to question what others mean when they resort to them.

Your choices

Achieving consistency in making choices starts with understanding that you have freedom of choice, and the decisions you make are yours, no one else's. When you fully appreciate this, you will project it in your speech and actions, regardless of how busy you may be.

In certain workshops I lead, I focus on the participants' speech. One of the words I listen for is 'must'. An executive who frequently uses 'must' or 'have to' does not feel in control of their agenda or choices. A more charismatic speaker will speak in terms of personal choice.

Compare how two different CEOs describe their schedule. One says, 'I have to be in Frankfurt on Wednesday and in Berlin on Thursday. I have an urgent meeting with our R&D Director before the weekend, so I must get on the 11am flight on Friday. If all goes according to plan, I hope to meet with him at 3 or 4pm at the latest.'

What is your impression of this CEO? Mine is that the executive has to be here, there and everywhere, and the words 'if' and 'hope' support the image that they are not in control of their very busy agenda. This CEO is driven by circumstance.

The second CEO says, 'I will be in Frankfurt on Wednesday and travel to Berlin on Thursday. As I will be returning on the 11am flight on Friday, this will allow sufficient time for a 4pm meeting with the R&D Director.'

In this version, the CEO's dynamic lifestyle sounds interesting. The projected decisiveness regarding the programme makes their choices sound like the right, manageable ones.

I recommend relegating the word 'must' to the disposal bin. Thinking and speaking in terms of having to do things zaps your energy, and may cause others to sympathise with you in a way that tends to erode esteem. Expressing freedom of choice is as important as the choice itself. There is a fundamental difference between doing something because it is your choice and doing something because you have to. You will project a stronger sense of personal leadership by saying what you will or intend to do.

Now that your vocabulary is richer for being one word poorer, how do you ensure your choices do not cause confusion or disengagement? To facilitate the process of being consistent in your approach, I have devised the following guidelines that I have divided into four clear criteria.

When you are faced with a choice, check that it meets the following criteria:

The choice is yours to make. Are you stepping into another person's area of responsibility? If so, let go and leave the choice where it belongs. Otherwise you could be taking unnecessary ownership, thereby undermining the other persons' authority, shrinking their responsibility or causing others to lose trust in you.

The choice is linked to the purpose of what you do and your added value. Make sure that the choice you face is relevant. If it is, move firmly and confidently to make the choice and underline your sincerity and credibility. If you are asked to make a choice that does not appear to be relevant, dig deeper to understand its origin before taking it on board or dismissing it.

The choice is related to agreed objectives. If you cannot explain your choice easily or relate it to the agreed objectives of the organisation, others will consider it to be in conflict with the envisaged result. It may even have a derailing effect. Choices without a clear context are the ones that tend to be questioned, reversed, regretted or undervalued.

The issue is clearly defined and you have tested assumptions. Testing assumptions is a crucial activity if issues that reach your desk are contentious and based on narrow findings. If the issue is clear and you have tested assumptions, the circumstances are right for you to make a choice. Otherwise, you need to get to the bottom of the real issue before acting. Ignoring this phase may jeopardise the validity of your choice and complicate rather than simplify the issue at hand.

> *A man who is at the top is a man who has*
> *the habit of getting to the bottom.*
> **Joseph E. Rogers**

In this section, did you notice that I have not used the word 'decision'? I chose to go with 'choice', and this is why:

As we build on a different kind of leadership suited to our fast-moving environment with a technology revolution and changing organisational structures and expectations at its core, focusing on choices leads to better results than focusing on decisions. Although both words are used inter-changeably, there are differences between the two, and I believe they call for a different approach.

Focusing on choices opens your mind. Choices suggest there are alternatives. This involves a mindset approach, meaning the choice is influenced by your values and beliefs, the contribution of others, and the knowledge that you have the opportunity and right to select the best way forward. Thinking in terms of choices allows you to check the four criteria outlined above.

Decision making, on the other hand, is a process orientation. It implies reaching a conclusion or resolution after analysing the facts and information. It does not suggest there are alternatives. Latin *decidere* literally means 'to cut off', from *de-* 'off' and *caedere* 'to cut'. Therefore, in making a decision, we go through steps to eliminate options. Thinking in terms of decisions can pull you into the decision-making process phase too soon, increasing the risk of inconsistencies and lack of relevant knowledge.

Energy management above time management

The third area of preparation is about developing a strong network of influence by being energy driven, not time driven; result driven, not action driven.

I believe that energy management makes more sense in a business context than time management. I have seen how my clients who apply the principles of energy management have increased their influence within their networks.

If we manage our energy, we focus on giving something a purpose before we decide to do it. Our time is not renewable, but our energy is. Applying energy management is indispensable for proactive leadership in dynamic environments. This is about achieving more value and results in less time, rather than doing more in less time.

I spoke of the risks of residing in an Efficiency Comfort Zone in Chapter One. New technology helps us to work faster, and working faster allows us to do more in less time. However, a work pattern that is based on increasing our time efficiency alone increases repetition in our daily work. There is less time to think of what we need to be doing as we concentrate on efficiency. We deal first with the easy things, such as e-mails or social media posts, whether they're relevant or not. Our new-found routine helps us to switch frequently between all platforms. The number of interruptions increases, but we are used to reacting quickly so we deal with them as we attempt to work on a more important and challenging project.

This time-driven approach will diminish our resourcefulness.

Now I will show you how you can change this work pattern. The greatest professional and personal rewards will come from choosing to focus on areas in which you will make the greatest difference. These rewards include increased influence, personal development and physical wellbeing.

Applying energy management in our networks

A good place to start applying energy management is in our networks. The greatest challenge we face today is how to gain maximum mutual benefit from our professional relationships. There is no doubt that customer relationship management is run on routine. Annual account plans are highly predictable and tend to focus on unit sales, margins, forecasts, marketing strategies and loyalty incentives. Personal relationships are an afterthought in this era of 'measurables'.

Relationships are the driver of progress, opportunities, innovation and profit. However, this has become a field of activity that managers play by ear or step into spontaneously from time to time when targets start slipping or competitors gain ground. Relationship management as an afterthought is noticeable from middle management through to the board. Without a strategy in this area, it is impossible for leaders to feel they are meeting the expectations of those in their network or benefiting sufficiently from the wealth of contacts that surrounds them. The result is that leaders use excessive energy and time trying to be a bit of everything to everyone.

Consider the following questions:

- Have you mapped all your stakeholders?

- Are you neglecting certain stakeholders and overindulging in your contacts with others?

- Are you a strategic partner or, in certain relationships, too pleasing?

- When did you last add a new dimension to a long-standing relationship?

- Do you apply more or less the same approach to all your contacts?

- Do you feel some parties expect too much of you and that others do not show enough interest?
- Do you exchange knowledge or do you share standard information of little added value with your suppliers or sponsors?

Getting this aspect of your business life right will be gratifying. I will demonstrate how you can use a diagram to visualise where you stand in relation to your many stakeholders.

The first step is to personalise your stakeholders. These are both internal and external parties who can influence or be affected by your actions, objectives and policies. Your family members are also stakeholders as they have an interest in what you do, but in this exercise we will limit stakeholders to your business-related contacts.

The best way to learn is by doing, so let's do an exercise to understand how you can put more purpose and value into expanding your network of influence.

The stakeholder chart depicts your network of influence and can be compared to a rotating wheel of progress. It has you at its core, surrounded by your stakeholders. You build success by adding value and mutual benefit to your relationship with each stakeholder. The more successful your relationships are, the more smoothly the wheel will turn, and as it turns, your reputation builds.

List your stakeholders and select eight whom you will include in the diagram. They may be groups (e.g. your Asian customers, your European customers, the Board of Directors, your management team, the HR Department, the Financial Department, your competitors, the media, shareholders) or individuals. When you have created your shortlist of stakeholders, put the name of each one in a separate section of the diagram.

Stakeholder Wheel

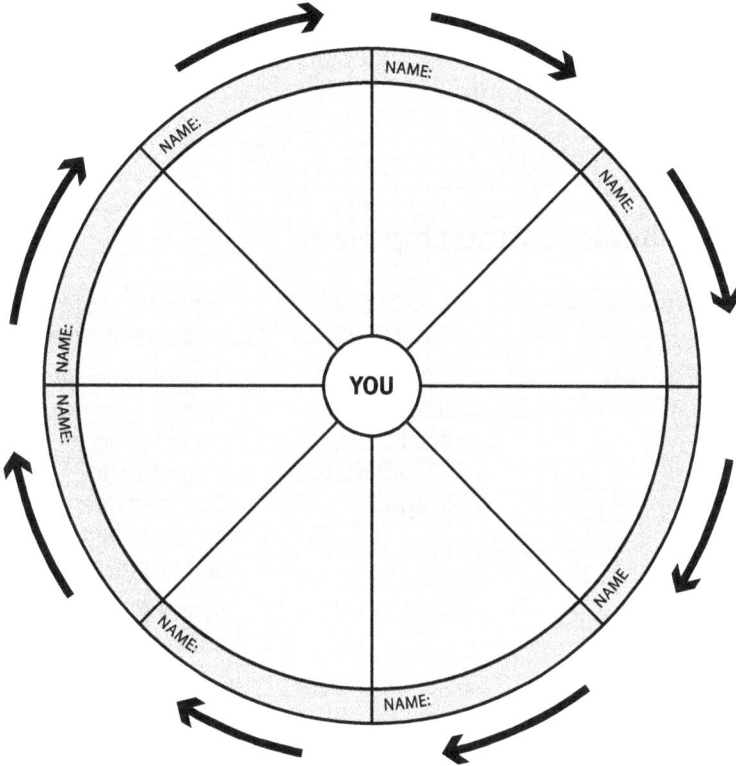

A copy of the stakeholder wheel can be downloaded from
http://www.jpcint.com/publications

You may decide to create a second circle so that you use one circle for your internal and one circle for your external stakeholders, bringing the number of stakeholders up to sixteen.

To get the wheel turning, we are going to give smart content to each section. Create a table with three columns and call it your Stakeholder Partnership Plan. The first column will list the names of your stakeholders. The second column will list what you wish to achieve in your relationship with each stakeholder in the coming twelve months to bring something new for real progress. The third column will list your actions/priorities to help you achieve the objectives in the second column.

Here's an example:

Stakeholder partnership plan

STAKEHOLDER	RELATIONSHIP OBJECTIVES	PRIORITIES FOR NEXT TWELVE MONTHS
ACZ, largest German supplier	Increase trust to achieve a better understanding of ACZ's culture and objectives More knowledge sharing on a strategic level Determine if ACZ could be the right partner for a joint venture with our subsidiary in Frankfurt	Change nature of meetings. Schedule a meeting once per quarter to discuss market developments and strategic responses Involve ACZ in innovation platform Create framework for better contact between both boards and middle management teams
Back office sales team	Increase their motivation, involvement and contact with other departments and clients Team takes on more responsibility	Include the team in off-site strategy session Visit offices once each month to increase their engagement Assess level of skills and ambition

STAKEHOLDER	RELATIONSHIP OBJECTIVES	PRIORITIES FOR NEXT TWELVE MONTHS
Management team (MT)	MT takes more initiative to improve processes MT builds awareness of external developments	Lead MT meetings differently. No more predictable 'update' meetings. Focus on external opportunities in relation to internal limitations Joint setting of progress objectives New topics: business model and organisational structure

Using the wheel of progress and creating a Stakeholder Partnership Plan will help you to focus on transforming the purpose and value of each relationship. In this manner you, instead of circumstances, drive the agenda.

Traditional stakeholder management plans tend to be unilateral action plans that focus specifically on achieving quantifiable results (e.g. 15% more business from a client). Past achievements and justifiable forecasts are the main considerations. I do not believe this type of stakeholder management to be sustainable in a fast-changing or disruptive business climate. All you need to do is focus on the third column of your stakeholder partnership plan to achieve an outstanding balance of energy investment in all your stakeholders. The only well-chosen activities that appear in the third column are those that support your relationship objectives in the second column. Limit yourself to these and you will save time while achieving more.

Activities that do not contribute to your objectives can be delegated to someone else. This way you will break ineffective patterns and channel the energy spent on stakeholders towards an exciting new outcome and progress. There are considerable time benefits as your agenda will be driven by predetermined priorities per stakeholder as opposed to ad hoc activities. You will focus only on activities that will build relevant and stronger relationships. Your priorities will be energising and related to a mutually beneficial purpose.

Let me end this section on one more benefit of developing your network of influence based on energy management. A reputation is generally dealt with as something that happens to people. It is often considered a question of luck that people run into kind, intelligent individuals who see how good they are and help build their reputation. It doesn't work that way.

In the business world today, we cannot afford to leave anything so crucial to chance. Your reputation is the total value of your relationships with your stakeholders. By adding value to your relationship with each stakeholder, you will automatically be building a sustainable reputation. It will multiply as the wheel turns and your stakeholders interact with their stakeholders.

Summary

Leadership styles should not be static, but evolve in harmony with the fast-moving changes in our business environment. As certain external changes are revolutionary, a leader cannot afford to rely on old navigation methods to weather new storms. Becoming a different kind of leader in specific areas can only be sustainable and effective if we first gain a thorough understanding of what will put us in a strong starting position.

We have studied three areas of leadership:

- Professional identity: think purpose, not profile
- Be consistent, not predictable
- Energy management above time management

You have given new meaning to your role, enabling you to position yourself well. You understand the fundamental difference between having a function and a purpose, and the essence of being consistent in the words you use and the choices you make. And to complete this section, you prepared for building a network of influence to fast-track progress.

The theme of the next chapter builds on from this one. We will now discuss the meaning of a different kind of leader on the job.

5

On the Job

We all live under the same sky,
but we don't all have the same horizon.
Konrad Adenauer

On the job, we are aware of what we like and don't like in our immediate environment, and what feels right and what needs to change. Yet, as a leader, where does one begin to bring about meaningful change in a fast-paced world where a short-term focus, firefighting, and dealing with an overload of information have become the accepted way of life? People don't feel good about working in this reactive manner, but we see all too often that it lasts for a relatively long period.

Being a different kind of leader in our dynamic world today is about influencing circumstances, not being driven by circumstances. It is about applying variation in our approach, conduct, patterns, and being aware of our biases.

In this chapter, I will zoom in on four areas in which I believe leadership transformation is required.

Diversity abroad, sameness at home?

Imagine you are flying to an unfamiliar destination. Visualise the business trip you are about to make. What will you do to prepare for that trip?

Is much of your time spent on:

- Reviewing the relationship with your business contact to date?
- Reading about the newly appointed members of their board or management team?
- Analysing their potential needs?
- Finding out about their relationship with your competitors?
- Evaluating past negotiations?
- Looking into their financial situation?
- Studying their market position, objectives and geographical area of business?
- Assessing the phase of the company and its key challenges?
- Preparing your PR material, offer and strategy?
- Defining your plan B?

All the above is valuable. But this is the predictable, routine part of preparing for a business trip abroad. Now let's take a wider-angle perspective.

If your trip was successful and you were confident it would lead to mid- and long-term benefits, then you probably spent more than 50% of your preparation time doing broader research. It is likely that you looked into a range of the following aspects:

- Your foreign contact's professional background
- Cultural specifics, including business and social etiquette, communication and leadership styles
- The country's history, economy and (recent) politics
- Regional tensions
- News items featuring prominently in local media channels
- Local sports heroes
- National holidays – religious, historical or political
- Societal or natural challenges and things of national pride

This is what would put you in a position to really connect with your business partner and see the richness of the differences between your cultures. You would have laid the groundwork to interact appropriately with the right finesse and respect, opening new doors at various levels. Thanks to this broader approach in preparing for a visit to a different environment, you would allow yourself to gain valuable insights during your stay. If you would use these insights in your subsequent proposal to your business partner, this would give them the assurance you had understood their culture and their needs.

FINDING COMMON GROUND

Let me share with you how I prepared for one of my trips to visit a steel company in Wales. I knew my greatest challenge would lie in my interviews with the company's factory workers, who were facing redundancies and great uncertainty.

I put much time into studying all the documentation the company sent to me, as well as the external market environment and circumstances that included many obstacles. Understanding the market, the challenges, both internal and external, the financial outlook and uncertainties gave me the basic knowledge I needed. But that, I knew, would not be enough for the factory workers and union members to open up to yet another consultant. So, I put much more time into studying the economic situation in the local community, gaining an understanding of the tensions and worries, the strength of the unions, and what united people. Zooming in on the last point is where I struck gold – sport. It just so happened that the 2015 Rugby World Cup was being hosted by England while I was in Wales, and some games were played at the Millennium Stadium in Cardiff.

I decided to become knowledgeable in the field of rugby. Even though I have a South African background, I was a novice when it came to the rules of the game. Within a few days, I knew the names of the prominent Welsh, English, South African and Australian players, and had mastered most of the jargon. I studied the pool results and which of the big matches were soon to be played.

Feeling the rugby excitement and being up to date on the winners and losers, I effortlessly connected with a cross-section of employees, regardless of their position and sentiments. I shared my shock with union members when Japan beat South Africa, considered the biggest upset in the history of rugby. They commiserated, and together we put our hopes on Wales against England, the match of the tournament. I can still feel the sheer joy of everyone in the company when Wales did beat England!

It was this out-of-the-ordinary research that allowed me to gain the trust and openness of the factory workers. Communication flowed as they shared concerns, ideas and grievances, because we had connected through what mattered most to them in October 2015: beating England during the Rugby World Cup.

Another method I use to get a better sense of the country or region I am visiting is to leave enough time to read the local newspaper in the hotel breakfast room before meeting with my clients. Thanks to reading the *Albanian Daily News* every morning when I was in Tirana in October 2017, I gained a much better understanding of the local challenges and circumstances. Mentioning a news item on a local celebrity was an excellent ice-breaker.

Leaders need to step back to evaluate and reflect on their performance prior to and during trips abroad. Could they strike a better balance between an approach driven by time, data and bottom-line results and an approach aimed at generating non-quantifiable benefits?

In our fast-paced business world, softer benefits are often not seen as worthy of serious consideration because there is no definitive way of measuring their worth. What monetary value can be attached to them? Students through to trainees, managers and top executives have been programmed to understand and build on financial objectives.

If, however, leaders broaden their perspectives, prepare differently for their encounters abroad, and see themselves as ambassadors whose actions, expressions of interest and interpersonal skills extend beyond the negotiation table, it will result in an unparalleled level of mutual understanding and respect. There is a role here for a different kind of leader – one who sets the example on how to be successful internationally in a world of increased competition, tension, uncertainty and complexity.

Imagine that a Company Director on a business trip visits a regional community project close to the heart of the local business partner. This would demonstrate that the Director is not only interested in closing a deal, but also in

understanding the local community and building a beneficial long-term relationship. What an impact that would have.
You may recall that I am in favour of companies having clear
foreign policies. Well they begin with this level of understanding which lays the groundwork for a longer term and
more resilient relationship.

The second point to consider is the extent to which the skills
leaders apply abroad are applied back home. After gaining
new experiences in a different environment and feeling
energised and intrigued by what they have experienced, too
many leaders return to their familiar working environments
and revert to business as usual. What do they see back at
headquarters? What they have seen before. Complacency
sets in. And then two months later, all their wonderful
preparation and curiosity are aroused once again because
it is time for the next trip.

To remain relevant as a leader tomorrow, our inquisitive
minds should not go into sleep mode when we are in our
familiar day-to-day environment. We need to maintain our
ability to observe and capitalise on differences, and understand the detriment of prolonged sameness. An inquisitive
mind is a leader's greatest personal asset. This entails applying the full spectrum of preparation and observation as we
apply to our trips abroad to our conduct, communication
and decision making back home. Observing with an open
mind can lead to us seeing new forces at work, identifying
opportunities and underused potential, and then acting on
what we see.

If a decision-making process stalls and drags on, this can be
because a leader is trying to change the mindsets of others,
while doing more of the same in unchanged settings. It is

far easier to change the decision-making settings than to change the minds of others. Different settings and new dynamics can build engagement and fast-track a process that was starting to suffocate.

Think too of how you consciously adapt your speech to connect with your business associates abroad. You probably speak more clearly, using short sentences and simple words, making sure that your messages match the interests or concerns of others. You are aware of timing, setting, sensitivities and the composition of the group before getting down to contractual negotiations.

How much effort do you put into changing your speech, conduct and the context of your messages in your day-to-day business environment? Do you adapt your message and its context to make maximum impact on different departments and influence employees with diverse cultural and professional backgrounds?

Remember how energised you were when you were abroad. To be successful, inject some of this energy and creativity into how you interact with your colleagues back home. You'll say farewell to sameness and build a smarter organisation.

The power of observation

One of the most revealing tests of a leader's effectiveness is their ability to make the right judgement calls in the face of a crisis. Equally important is their ability to act wisely when there is no crisis to facilitate change, increase creativity or enhance engagement. The charisma and calm control that a leader projects when making decisions and presiding over high-risk issues are paramount for generating support and leading by example.

I touched on the importance of observation in the previous section. In this section, we will turn observation into an indispensable skill to broaden our perspectives and cope successfully with speed, unforeseen developments and unprecedented levels of complexity.

Never underestimate the power of observation. It helps us to take a bird's-eye view of circumstances and developments for sound decision making. It is the art of watching with the purpose of learning and the benefit of defeating our biases for better outcomes and personal progress. There is no limit to what we can observe. Think of the interaction between two colleagues, how a change initiative is received, the dynamics of meetings, and how a client responds to a new service.

Leaders need to respond successfully to the consequences of new organisational structures, changing business models, ongoing digitalisation, the use of big data and new team formats. This requires the ability to develop insights in pace with changing circumstances, which cannot be achieved without the routine of targeted observation. Neither can a deeper level of understanding and critical thinking be obtained without this skill followed by reflection.

Without this practice of observation and reflection, leaders cannot have the added value to warrant their positions in an era that is moving towards the sophistication of self-managed teams. With attention spans being short and information readily available to employees across the board, leaders demonstrate their immeasurable value if their conduct is aimed at building capacity, making connections and setting direction in an evolving manner.

Observation is not simply looking and seeing. Before I describe how to observe effectively to develop knowledge and insights, let us look at four common biases that apply in some measure to most leaders.

Tangible results outclass process. There is a tendency to attach far more importance to the results of a project than to the process that led to the results. This narrow focus on the outcome limits learning experiences. Less obvious opportunities are not identified. We discussed how management by objectives, if narrowly applied, facilitates unethical behaviour. If a leader does not show interest in the process, this hampers creative thinking, caps potential and encourages cutting corners.

Narrow focus – familiar above unfamiliar. Do you show more interest in what is familiar to you than in foreign, unfamiliar terrain? Some leaders seek to reach a quick solution and an efficiently achieved outcome while restricting the options and possible outcomes to those most familiar to them. People who speak about something the leader recognises get more attention than those who speak on topics that trigger uncertainties. Are you spending more time with like-minded colleagues than with colleagues who are likely to shed a different light on existing issues and new opportunities?

Short-term benefits are more highly rewarded than long-term benefits. Do you express more appreciation for short-term results than for initiatives that will produce sustainable results in the future? Inconsistencies in what leaders expect and reward stand in the way of a team adopting strategies for a mid- to long-term vision. Leaders don't get what they truly want for ongoing development and a bigger competitive advantage if they rejoice at quick wins and show little interest during development and planning phases.

Confirmation bias. This bias pops up when leaders do not have an open mind. It need not necessarily be structural; it could occur when pressures on a leader increase and they consider more ideas and alternatives to be inconvenient. This is when leaders look for and find evidence that confirms their views. They will ignore facts that do not confirm they are right.

There are many examples of this bias. If we only read articles and log into news channels that give us the views we like to hear, we are looking for confirmation of our opinions and missing other perspectives.

REDIRECT THE SPOTLIGHT TO FOCUS ON YOUR AUDIENCE

By observing, we are able to take a step back, remove ourselves from our (subconscious) biases and be intrigued by what we discover. So how is it done?

Some years ago, I was invited to lead an interactive session on future planning for postgraduate students at Erasmus University in Rotterdam. To my surprise, the lighting changed as soon as I arrived on the stage. I was in a weak position, standing on the brightly lit stage with 500 students in front of me enjoying a semi-dark and relaxing atmosphere. I knew then that I would not be able to respond to the interests and questions of the students if I remained showcased.

After I intervened, the technicians lit up the hall and reduced the intensity of the light on me. I was now able to speak while focusing on the audience. I attribute the success of the lecture to this physical and psychological change of setting.

If we use this 'redirect the spotlight' example not in a literal way but as a metaphor, it is equally effective. It means we are not obsessed by our own thoughts, convictions, the need to claim space and make a point as soon as possible. Rather, we use our skills to hear what really matters to other people before conveying a much-improved message. Our focus is on them, not on ourselves. Redirecting the spotlight is the fastest way for speakers and presenters to gain confidence.

The competence of tuning into those around us is required for effective observation. By observing, we open our minds to thoughts other than our own, experiences that are new to us, and options that we hadn't considered. This is where we are able to rise above our biases, whatever they may be. It allows us to read the currents, control our emotions, enjoy a high level of credibility and be smarter at testing assumptions.

With shortcuts looming, the fast proliferation of compromised information and the need to analyse data effectively for better decisions, we need to test assumptions in an astute manner. To do this well, we let go of what we think is correct in order to listen first to those around us.

Through careful consideration and observation, you will know which questions to ask, but here are some tips to get you started:

- Always define in advance precisely what you will be observing
- Stipulate the purpose of your observation – why is it important to you?
- Consciously observe only one thing at a time

- Where (i.e. under which circumstances) will you observe this topic and when will you do this?
- What will you do with the outcome after some extended reflection?

Imagine that you have discovered a lack of knowledge sharing between two senior managers. The consequences of this could be significant. You could test your assumption by asking both managers if this is indeed the case and risk a superficial conversation filled with denials, maybes, indifference or accusations. Or you could observe first, then base a more worthwhile conversation on your observations.

By answering the questions above, you would develop a plan of action that is simple and effective:

- I will observe the interaction between the two managers in different settings
- The purpose of my observation is to find out if there is strained communication between them in areas demanding transparency and dialogue
- I will observe how they respond to one another
- The settings of my observation will be the board meeting this week and the off-site strategy session next week
- I will confront both managers with my observations in order to obtain an explanation and their subsequent plan of action to improve matters

My advice to every leader is to consciously observe something every week. It is always best to alternate between internal and external observations to maintain a healthy balance. The outcome of all the observations will form a powerful agenda of priorities and prompt intervention when it matters.

It is easy to spot a person who tunes in to the environment and builds insights in a steady manner. It is the one who sits down at a departure gate, on a terrace or in a hotel lobby and does not reach instantly for a device. Instead, they look around, appear to be in control, are present and aware.

To complete this section, I recommend that leaders encourage younger employees to develop this skill of observation followed by reflection. It will improve their development and make them more valuable to your organisation. Gaining access to extensive data is one thing, but being able to interpret data intelligently is a different matter altogether. Being able to make sense out of an overload of data starts with the ability to observe and reflect.

Role model in a time of disruption

This is the third area requiring a different approach. But how relevant is the notion that leaders should be role models in diminishing or transitioning hierarchical structures?

We live in a time of complexity and uncertainty, accelerated technological advancement, and declining confidence in media, politicians and businesses. Business models, organisational structures and work processes continue to change. We also have the relatively new social media-related phenomena of fake news and post-truth. Fake sound was added to this in 2017. I was listening to a BBC broadcast and heard Barack Obama's voice. His words surprised me, but after a few minutes of puzzlement I realised I had tuned into a programme on synthetic voice sound. Technology has advanced to be able to match synthetic voice imitations perfectly. This may now mean that we will need to check the source of audio recordings before we can trust their validity.

Now, more than in any preceding decade, an organisation needs a role model. The ultimate achievement for any leader is to be considered a role model, even though the modesty of true leaders would not allow them to claim this label.

Being a role model begins with awareness and choice. An awareness of the behaviour you demonstrate and whether it is the behaviour you would like to see multiplied throughout the organisation and reflected back at you. Choice because qualifying as a role model doesn't happen by chance, even if you have the required skills and natural ability.

In today's fast-paced business environment, where ethical and strategic dilemmas are never far away, there are too many situations in which costly judgement errors can be made. Choosing to lead by example can help us to think first and take values and objectives into consideration; to maintain a bird's-eye view of situations; to respond in tune with the importance of the matter at hand; to acknowledge errors and take appropriate actions. Becoming a role model doesn't happen automatically for the vast majority of people in business.

Leading by example is all about the inseparable combination of what and how. I remember leading a masterclass on Global Business Development in Amsterdam. It was 4pm – a tricky time of day to keep the attention of a large group of business people. To pre-empt the possibility of an afternoon dip, I opened the session by getting everyone to stand up and sing along to Bananarama's version of the well-known song, 'It Ain't What You Do (It's The Way That You Do It)' as its lyrics refer to the way, time and place that you do it being the important criteria to succeed.

Being a role model is all about the way in which something is done, the timing and the setting. In this section, I will focus on four topics that relate to being a role model.

- The use of big data
- Image and reputation management
- Mindset
- Moral leadership

These topics require the visible leadership skills that generate respect and build stronger team members at all levels; the skills that ensure there is always a bridge between newly gained insights on the one hand and the wisest way to apply these on the other.

The use of big data

What could be more relevant than this topic today? We now have unprecedented data-processing power, and there are many examples in different industries where considerable authority has been given to computer algorithms.

However, using artificial intelligence is a means to enhance, not replace a leader's path to drawing conclusions or making decisions. What machines can produce in a methodical way is valuable. What machines do not replace is the thinking that humans use to reach inventive outcomes or persuade others. It is the use of creativity and norms and values that machines cannot offer.

As a leader, encourage employees to monitor, manage and interpret data by using common sense. A leader should ask questions regarding the purpose of the data, how it relates to certain objectives, the value of the findings, and how they will be used. Leaders who ask these questions build awareness in their organisations of how best to use digital tools to grow the business. Generating the right data and knowing how to interpret it is considered by many business consultants to be as important as the company's core products or services.

It is the leader's task to ensure the organisation's employees know exactly what the problem is that needs to be solved. Without this starting point, data will be used indiscriminately. The leader's behaviour should be consistent with the viewpoint that data supports rather than drives decisions.

Pitfalls to watch for are:

- Sending projects into the organisation for further analysis without determining a crystal-clear purpose and meaningful context
- Focusing predominantly on short-term analyses as opposed to longer term opportunities that are more externally focused
- Allowing data analyses to determine customers' needs

Head office can establish a competitive advantage when it develops business policies, conducts analyses, makes marketing improvements, revises price policies and upgrades products. However, these activities are far removed from interaction with customers. A competitive advantage that is dependent on these activities will be short-lived as competitors are quick to copy what the market leader does well.

To establish a more sustainable advantage, organisations must pay as much attention to innovation of their sales strategy as to innovation of their products. Insight-based selling has become a widely-used term, mainly because customers have access to such a broad scope of information that they do not feel confident about making the right choices. To build loyalty, offer customers the added value they are looking for today – new ideas and perspectives concerning the use of your services as well as insights into new market opportunities. Data supports this process, but cannot lead it.

Build partnerships by interacting with customers on a personal level, asking the right questions and sharing knowledge that helps them to grow their businesses. It is here where customers' needs, including the decisive softer category of requirements, are identified.

I encourage leaders to ensure that they highlight to their staff the value of real conversation with clients, despite the easier option of online chats and use of computer generated answers. One need not exclude the other. While we embrace the technology of artificial intelligence we must ensure we retain sufficient variation in how we communicate. 'Easy' has never been the fastest way to achieve the most rewarding outcomes. We need to add new, less predictable activities to customer-supplier relationships each year and alternate between communication styles in order to enhance these relationships and learn what numbers alone cannot tell us. This will help us to gain a deeper understanding of the market's needs prior to using additional digital tools to calculate potential or quantify actual demand.

When two suppliers have similar products and services within an acceptable price range, they generally make the unfortunate choice to compete on price; a destructive policy of discounting sets in. If a procurement manager were to ask, 'What else can you offer me to make your offer more attractive than that of your competitor?', what would your initial reaction be? Too often, suppliers presume the procurement manager is looking for a discount. In fact, 'What else can you offer me?' refers first and foremost to added value. Inviting your customers to join one of your knowledge platforms will help them to gain a better understanding of trends relevant to them, and this makes you an invaluable business partner. It is this unexpected personal benefit that will help a procurement manager choose between companies with similar services within an acceptable price range.

Growth comes from thinking and acting beyond routine as we set direction and devise policies, use data smartly, apply human judgement and allow machines to do the work requiring meticulous accuracy. If this means redefining our roles, this would indicate progress.

Image and reputation management

This topic applies both to leaders and their organisations. It requires of the leader a high level of awareness and proactive steering. Reputational damage can have far-reaching consequences, as many high-profile scandals have shown. Building an organisation with an excellent reputation starts with the leader's personal image. A question to ask is, 'Do my priorities and conduct accentuate the kind of leader I want to be?' Answering questions like the ones listed below may help you to identify possible pitfalls.

- If I believe in balancing my focus between internal and external developments and being able to get to the core of complex matters, does this conflict with my tendency to micromanage?

- If I would like to be recognised for good listening and questioning skills, does it make sense that I react to my phone's every beep or ring when I am in meetings?
- If I wish to appear in control of circumstances and my agenda, is this compatible with looking rushed and being consistently late for appointments?
- If I intend to project a healthy image, would it make sense to be known for a habit of sending late night messages?
- If I praise the value of diversity, would I build credibility if I were to underuse the existing opportunities for diversity within the organisation?

The key word here is consistency. Trust is hard earned.

We discussed stakeholder partnerships in Chapter Four. Establishing a strong personal reputation is about being committed to executing our plans regarding the specific objectives, approach and actions that we devised for each of our stakeholders. Personal reputations are fragile. Therefore, developing a positive image and a reputation to match that image will have to become second nature to leaders today. Only then can they move up the corporate ladder and maintain high-profile positions in competitive environments without enduring costly reputation dents that could include being publicly shamed.

Let's now look at the organisation's image and reputation. This is a topic of anxiety for many leaders at a time when social media platforms can disrupt reputations and carefully designed marketing and PR campaigns. Building and maintaining a company reputation has evolved into an area of business that requires constant attention, agile thinking, multidisciplinary involvement and quick responses. Getting to grips with how to manage this development is where many leaders stumble.

We cannot control how the market will express its experiences or opinions concerning our organisations. Add to this the fact that risks related to reputation management can also come from within the organisation. Employees can display impulsive behaviour that reflects badly on the organisation.

This is a common pattern: an organisation receives positive comments on social media channels through earned media (i.e. media coverage not paid for by the organisation). This sends waves of excitement through the organisation and there is impatience to get more. Employees understand all too well that statements of wide public interest trigger a lively stream of comments that puts the company and themselves in the limelight. Some impulsively share sensitive company information and personal views. Consumers who detect either embarrassing or highly inappropriate business practice then enjoy making it go viral.

In addition to unrestrained employee behaviour, there is a risk that the organisation as a whole may give unintentional impressions on social media. This could be due to inconsistencies in communication or as a result of the company ignoring certain legal or strategic restrictions before posting news items.

All of the above calls for a social media policy to ensure senior executives do not have to meticulously guard the use of social media. Rather, a leader should prioritise the development and implementation of a policy that provides clarity and guidelines for optimal use of this powerful communications medium. Guidelines need to include the involvement of different disciplines or departments such as risk, compliance and marketing. There should be contingency plans in place to ensure there is no delay in response when mistakes are made. Dealing with mistakes in a convincing and prompt manner will lead to positive word of mouth.

A leader's role here is to ensure that a multidisciplinary team designs and reviews a social media policy that evolves in tandem with changing circumstances. The leader also ensures that processes, including companywide knowledge sharing, are in place to safeguard broad implementation and understanding of the policy. Without a social media policy in place, leaders will tend to micromanage the correction of mistakes and become overcautious.

Mindset

To be considered a role model, a leader will need to show evidence of an exemplary mindset. This topic could fill a separate book, so to simplify matters let me share my shortlist of mindset features that I believe breed success, based on many years of working with and observing members of executive boards.

Growth vs limitation mentality. Leaders with a growth mentality stand out in more ways than one. They are keen to share knowledge, recognition, decision making and the benefits of success with others. They believe in synergy and the economics of diversity. They demonstrate in their conduct that success can have a multiplying effect.

Complimenting others and removing barriers that limit their progress come naturally to a leader with a growth mentality. Faced with choices, if they lean towards a yes, they want to know more and ask sharp questions. If they are more inclined to think no, they test assumptions to learn before deciding. They do not believe there is a ceiling to success, neither do they see risks in acknowledging the contributions made by colleagues. Their choice of words reveals personal confidence and that they do not feel threatened by others. Success generates more success.

Tell-tale signs of a limitation mentality are shown in how a leader negotiates. They are inclined to choose at best a win-lose approach. It is likely that they delegate tasks without authority, mainly because they do not want to risk having colleagues encroaching on their turf. They are specialists in sharing information as opposed to insightful knowledge regarding policies or lessons learned.

Leaders who are this way inclined are more likely to experience stress and enter into restrictive dialogue. They believe that there is only one pie to be shared between all, and that giving a big section of the pie to one person would mean less for everyone else. Success does not multiply for the limitation mentality people; it diminishes as the number or impact of participants increases. People who are hostage to this mentality find it difficult to share credit or be genuinely pleased for the success of others.

I do not believe there are many role models who have a limitation mentality. When circumstances spiral out of control, the leader with a growth mentality is more likely to weather the storm than the leader with a limitation mentality.

Optimism and humour. Something that has struck me throughout my years working as a consultant is that there is one trait virtually all outstanding leaders have in common: a sense of humour. I did not expect to find this trait in countries that had endured much hardship, including (internal) wars, economic struggle, a lack of democratic freedom and stringent hierarchical organisational structures, but even in these countries, the most exemplary leaders were those who projected optimism. They were able to see the humour in situations and take a light-hearted approach to fixing a derailment. This quality allowed them to take ownership of their own responses and choices to use all resources available to them to solve a crisis. These leaders were successful in transitioning to a new economic order, and continue to reform their companies.

Multiple studies spanning multiple countries have suggested that positive work cultures have a considerable effect on productivity and profitability. A large part of having a positive work culture is having an optimistic, humorous leader. I am not suggesting that those with a stern, introvert demeanour take a crash course in joke telling or stand-up comedy. Besides, jokes often don't translate well from one culture to another. Simply smiling more or showing appreciation for an amusing story will help leaders to radiate calmness and competency in the face of challenges. An optimistic outlook is highly contagious.

Lifelong learning. Change has existed since the beginning of time. The difference in this world of disruption is the pace of development, supported by artificial intelligence. Therefore, leaders and employees are having to adapt at a much faster pace. All eyes are on the most senior executives as colleagues register how they adapt to disruption and rise above the challenges it brings.

Leaders who have a lifelong learning mindset are not fazed by new technologies and changing demands. A leader demonstrates this lifelong learning approach by using the skills that are needed to have a clear understanding of relevant challenges, possible solutions, international developments, strategic opportunities and risks. Understanding how artificial intelligence works and benchmarking will become important areas of focus.

Leaders need to take time out to be briefed by experts, attend seminars, invite specialists in different fields to be guest speakers at company functions, listen attentively to employees and customers, and above all make sure that relevant, future-focused training is provided to employees in order to champion a lifelong learning culture.

Stanford psychologist Carol Dweck speaks of learn-it-alls and know-it-alls. The know-it-alls often start out with more profession-related knowledge and a better education giving them an academic advantage above a percentage of their colleagues. However, the learn-it-alls who catch up quickly are likely to overtake the know-it-alls. This supports the quote: 'A students work for B students at companies founded by C students'.

Mental resilience. If I were to describe a leader who consciously builds mental resilience, I would say that they retain their balance through tough times. Such leaders remain focused and determined to succeed despite the difficulties they encounter. They learn from their mistakes and accept the mistakes others make, as long as those people learn from them too. Dealing effectively with setbacks and disappointments is an area in which mental resilience is strengthened.

A big item in this respect is emotional maturity. Mentally resilient leaders manage their emotional responses. Leaders who retaliate after receiving critical questions are not able to separate their emotions from the issue at hand. Emotional maturity is a requirement if leaders want to be kept in the loop, receive honest assessments, and read the undercurrents in the organisation.

It is crucial that we train our mental resilience by applying self-motivational tools and techniques to gain inspiration, positive thoughts and energy when they are needed most. Stepping out of a negative situation in order to look at it differently requires courage but will, in many cases, lead to the ability to change the game plan for a better outcome. When coaching professionals to become effective negotiators, I find that resilience is where they gain the biggest benefit. The most advanced and effective negotiating methods require that the leader knows how to appeal to the right needs and emotions. Leaders who are driven by emotion and extrinsic motivation such as fame, money and praise are unable to apply constructive interventions during negotiations. Neither are they able to take each stage of the negotiation a step further by keeping mutual interests in mind.

Moral leadership – the three-way principle

*Leaders get out in front and stay there by raising
the standards by which they judge themselves –
and by which they are willing to be judged.*
Frederick W. Smith, CEO of FedEx

133

Breakthrough technologies continue to open new doors to unlimited opportunity. This is happening in every sector from business services to medicine, space research and everything in between. Moral questions concerning the use of medical know-how, social instability, globalisation and protectionism, the upsurge of populism, and cybersecurity define a large part of a CEO's complex external environment. We have seen high-profile examples of unethical behaviour in various industries across continents, both in the public and private sectors. Such examples have led to increased public distrust of senior managers, in particular those representing large corporations. It is, therefore, not surprising that there is a growing need for organisations' stakeholders to see evidence of the CEO as a moral leader. People want to feel proud to be associated with an organisation with which they are closely connected either as a business partner, employee, investor, supplier or customer.

> *Trust is a serious problem; we have to get to a new level of transparency – only through radical transparency will we get to radical new levels of trust.*
> **Marc R. Benioff, Chairman and Chief Executive Officer, Salesforce, USA**

Moral leadership needs constant attention for three reasons. First of all, even if a leader is intrinsically moral and values-driven, these qualities may not be sufficiently observable to others. Morals and values need to be applied and demonstrated in an explicit and visible manner in order to influence the sentiments of critical stakeholders. Secondly, the complexity of our environment has an impact on internal affairs, too. Leaders are faced with difficult choices as well as intricate issues that are directly or indirectly linked to a range of projects, interests and people. There are grey areas in which the right path to take may not be clear-cut. Last but not least, there is less and less time in which to make the right judgement calls.

These circumstances have driven the need for CEOs and their executive teams to make corporate social responsibility (CSR) a well-structured core activity. The CEO's agenda has to change to balance profit making with activities that benefit society. Working for a moral organisation is increasingly a decisive factor for Millennials. The more CSR becomes integrated in an organisation's core policies, the more appealing the organisation becomes in a competitive job market.

It becomes easier to make CSR a sustainable core activity if social initiatives are closely linked to the organisation's purpose and operations. Employees' contributions to less privileged communities through sharing their knowledge and expertise can be integrated into the organisation's operations. Examples are computer-related education, technical support for communities aiming to become self-supporting, small business counselling, or vocational support for disadvantaged young people. Environmental initiatives and the selection of charities and volunteering projects should be designed and coordinated in such a way that they are manageable for the organisation, involve all employees and benefit the organisation's stakeholders. CSR includes ethical employment practices, from fair terms of employment, employee development, upscaling of skills, and career mobility to facilitating increased involvement and engagement.

I have discovered that executives can struggle to make difficult decisions that will receive sufficient support on the one hand and pre-empt lengthy debate or cynicism on the other. It is for this reason that I created the 3-Anchors Model to serve as a practical guideline for daily use. It helps to turn the big topic of moral leadership into a useful decision-making tool.

Take a look at the three anchors – transparency, fairness and respect – that together test the justifiability of a leader's decisions, actions and viewpoints. If an imminent decision passes this test, convey it to others in a manner that communicates not only the benefits and projected results, but also the moral context. Without this context, the leader increases their vulnerability and risks inconsistency and the loss of credibility.

3-Anchors Model

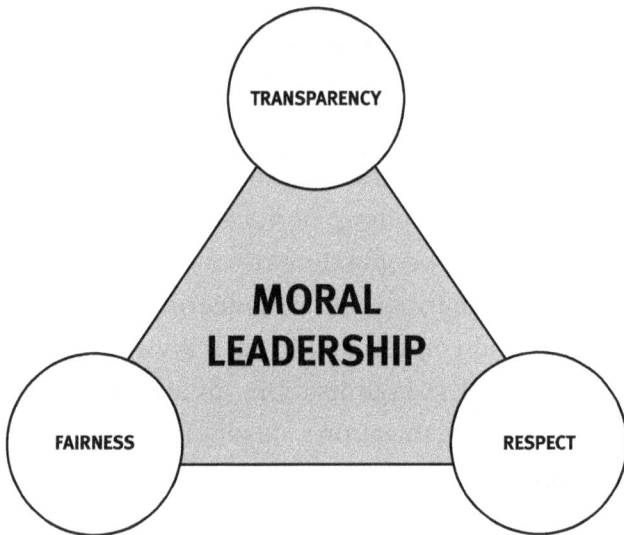

The questions to ask are:

- Will I be prepared to provide **transparency** regarding my motivations?

- Is this approach, viewpoint, action or decision **fair** to those involved?
- Is it **respectful** of the organisation's values and existing agreements?

The 3-Anchors Model

Let me give you an example. A frustration that I hear time and again concerns the way in which senior positions are filled. Frequently this is a closed-door procedure, and it is not uncommon for the right kind of communication to be lacking when it comes to selection processes, criteria and appointments. Therefore, those who have any interest in the outcome of the selection process will create their own reasoning.

Do any of these statements sound familiar to you?

- She was chosen because they needed to hit gender targets
- Not surprising, he has always been the CEO's protégé
- He is smart at office politics
- She knows which people to impress
- He made a clever move getting into line for that vacancy

Notice how none of these remarks suggests the person selected for the position is capable, a sensible choice or someone who brings valuable skills or experience to the job. Even if the candidate is the right choice, the process itself suggests that the leader's actions failed the 3-Anchors test. What do others see? Not the choice of candidate, but the flawed process.

Nepotism, the power of the inner circle, the old boys' network, a rigged procedure and other such disqualifications will start to chip away at the leader's image and widen the trust gap.

Transparency. There was none.

Fairness. The process was unfair to those who were not selected, and was particularly unfair to the person who was selected for the position. Having to disappoint employees from time to time is all part of normal business life. However, the impact is completely different if it is anchored in fair business practice.

Respect. The process suggested there was no respect for the ambition, anticipation, commitment and engagement of those hoping to be selected for the position. By choosing a closed-door procedure, the leader completely disregarded two of the company's values, which stipulated open communication and equal opportunity.

There is no place for the perception of a hidden agenda in moral leadership. If the leader runs through the 3-Anchors Model, they will be much more inclined to share the moral context of their decision. Having all points – transparency, fairness and respect – clarified upfront transforms the communication process and helps everyone understand the outcome. If it proves impossible to answer all three of the questions in an acceptable manner, then the leader knows in advance that the potential choice is the wrong one.

Let me close this chapter by sharing with you part of a recent conversation that I had with a business acquaintance. He told me that he had experienced a steep decline in his trust in the Board of Directors. Two phrases used by the directors remained engrained in his memory.

The first was that the organisation should 'sweat their resources' to improve bottom-line results. He could not reconcile this statement with the annual report saying the organisation's human resources were its most valued assets. The second point was the unashamed use of the term 'plausible deniability' to warrant bending the rules to achieve targets.

Plausible deniability is the ability of people (typically senior officials in a formal or informal chain of command) to deny knowledge of or responsibility for any damnable actions committed by others in an organisational hierarchy because of a lack of evidence that can confirm their participation, even if they were personally involved in or at least wilfully ignorant of the actions.
Wikipedia

These phrases, 'sweat our resources' and 'plausible deniability', unequivocally fail the 3-Anchors test of moral leadership: transparency, fairness and respect.

I encourage you to apply the 3-Anchors Model in every aspect of your business life. Without a helpful moral compass, tough decisions and dilemmas may weigh heavily on your shoulders, and may make you hesitate at a time when you need to make decisions.

Summary

Being on the job in this world of disruption demands that leaders do certain things differently. We made those things concrete in this chapter and broke big topics down into practical examples, exercises and tools, highlighting four key areas of competency in which leaders in all sectors can increase their influence significantly.

The first is that leaders should apply the same skills they use in international settings to their conduct back home in their local business environments.

The second area is developing and using the skill of advanced observation and reflection to set an agenda of priorities and interventions.

The third significant area of leadership we studied is what it takes to be considered a role model today:

- The intelligent use of big data
- Image and reputation management and the use of social media
- Effective mindsets
- Moral leadership

We then considered the fourth pillar of being a role model – being a moral leader – by examining the true meaning of moral leadership.

Finally, you became acquainted with my 3-Anchors Model, to be used in every business setting.

6

Teams Today – the Most Common Limitations

*More important than the quest for certainty
is the quest for clarity.*
François Gautier

Spotting the limitations in team performance and under-standing how they impact on company climate are the first steps to identifying an alternative approach to leading teams. A well-known African proverb says, 'If you want to go fast, go alone. If you want to go far, go together.' I often hear managers say, 'I know I should delegate this, but it will be done ten times quicker if I do it myself.' That may be a short-term gain, but teams don't flourish under a leader who holds on to delegable tasks.

Another broadly adopted belief is that leaders succeed best when they help others to succeed. However, it can be difficult for some leaders to put this into practice if their personalities or mindsets get in the way of letting others shine or experience accelerated learning opportunities.

If there is one area in the business world that is filled with dilemmas and challenges today, I would say it is team leadership. Dilemmas occur because teams are evolving structures, and more than ever before, they tend to want to evolve faster than company leadership structures, processes and policies. Also, there are many more first-time situations that team leaders face in this world of disruption. Changing dynamics and unforeseen developments can lead to misperceptions and unrealistic expectations.

These are common dilemmas that leaders face:

- Delegate it or do it myself?
- Maintain a professional, formal relationship with my team or encourage familiarity in settings that are becoming more and more informal?
- How to balance structured co-operation within and between teams with disorganised forms of team collaboration?
- Which communication format should I use?
- Surveillance of staff: what is permitted, and when can I use available data on employees' behaviour to intervene or apply corrective measures?
- How should I adapt my communication style when meeting with a global team?

These will remain tough questions for any leader until they redefine a) what the organisation's teams of the future should look like, and b) the strategy to get there.

Leaders and their teams form an emotional powerhouse. Let's start with leaders. When my clients have shown significant emotion, it has often been in relation to the performance of their teams on which they so heavily depend. Disappointment regarding colleagues who do not pull their weight or undermine new initiatives. Frustration when colleagues do not share important experiences and mistakes are repeated. Anger when requests are blatantly ignored. Surprise when a colleague rises to a challenge. Fear when a costly mistake is made. Joy when team co-operation leads to an outstanding performance.

Teams are environments in which ambitious leaders set the bar high regarding targets and expectations. Leaders see their teams as an extension of their own professional identities.

The emotional make-up of any team has an impact on the value of its co-operation, engagement, commitment and (financial) performance. Therefore, we should not under-estimate the need for leaders to understand the emotional status of their local or global teams.

Getting to grips with and influencing the emotional status of any team requires that leaders frequently engage with team members to read and understand the undercurrents in the team and wider organisation. Leaders may choose to stimulate certain emotions and weaken others to build a healthy work climate. Narcissistic leaders on the other hand can easily destroy morale by having no regard for the feelings, self-respect or contribution of others.

Given the importance of effective teams, we need to look at what their most common limitations are today. Which restrictive patterns hamper progress?

The over-analysed team

In their quest to strengthen their teams, organisations have not hesitated to pursue different avenues. Analytical tools such as personality tests have been applied for many decades. Ongoing developments in neuroscience and research have led to new insights and improvements in methods to produce even more accurate analyses of personality styles.

As leaders understand the growing importance of well-functioning teams in a turbulent world, it is not surprising that analytical tools are used systematically throughout organisations in all countries of operation. Many of these tools are freely available online and help individuals to identify their behavioural patterns, Jung personality types, and weakest and strongest traits. Restrictive behavioural habits are exposed, and more extensive reports will include prognoses such as future leadership capacity.

I am licensed to use two brand-name personality tests and I certainly recognise their added value. However, I also consider them to be of little value if they are not interpreted well and used effectively. Leaders must ensure that these analyses do not emphasise differences that divide people. Instead, they should encourage teams to recognise, understand and benefit from those differences. Secondly, they are a helpful support, but not a primary decision-making tool.

COLOUR-CODING

In the summer of 2017, I was invited to run a full-day workshop for a business development team. The participants were mainly outgoing people who conversed with ease and confidence. When we addressed the positioning of their team and their co-operation

with different departments and regions, the conversation sud-
denly turned very colourful. Colours were an indication of the
departments' most natural behaviour, from fast-paced decision
makers to analytical specialists. Department heads were said to
be red, mainly blue, too green or yellow. Frictions were explained
by clashing colours, not the cause of the friction. The participants
believed it was understandable that they struggled to communicate with back office support staff who, 'sadly for them', did not
have much blue or yellow in their profiles.

Soon after that workshop, I met a manager who had recently
joined the organisation. He, too, had undergone the profile test
and was relieved to be told his colour combination was fine for a
senior position. This also concerned him, though, as too much of
the same behaviour in middle and senior management positions
may feed the limiting phenomenon of 'groupthink'.

This demonstrates how any widely-used profile test can have
a limiting effect on the advancement of teams. If assessments
are used mainly to label yourself and others, then they
stereotype. The identified differences can be used by teams
as an excuse instead of an opportunity to build bridges and
gain knowledge. The true value of analytical tools starts
when differences are used to drive progress and synergy.

Research shows that tests in general have attached too
much value to where candidates' interests lie, based on the
assumption that interest equals ability. It does not. It certainly helps if candidates are genuinely interested in areas
of expertise that the organisation is seeking, but possessing
a skill takes more than the desire to possess it.

Only with a clear purpose and strategy as to how to use
profile insights to build strong teams can real change take
place. I believe this applies in equal measure to off-site

team building events and training programmes. If leaders focus on immediate improvements and create a framework that supports the learning, research shows that teams feel encouraged and engaged for a considerable time after such sessions. Unfortunately, too often leaders do not fulfil this role. Too much training can then result in individuals holding a cynical view of the leader's and the team's willingness and ability to change. The most talented and ambitious employees may jump ship.

An overload of unchannelled co-operation

Traditional lines of communication are disappearing, the number of management layers is decreasing, and global connectivity is increasing. Departments can no longer work in comfortable seclusion, unbothered by other areas of discipline.

A reason for the recent wave of restructuring within organisations is the need to do away with restrictive silos, cut costs and increase efficiency. Without silos, a broad-based form of co-operation is possible. Multiple departments are involved in different cycles of a company's products and services. For example, product development, marketing, sales and IT are just four departments that are involved in creating and delivering an integrated service to meet clients' needs in highly competitive markets. Therefore, the number of stakeholders who have an interest in any manager's work has multiplied.

Just picture the number of people who have an interest in an app for use by customers globally. Instead of listing the departments who need to know, we could list those who would not be involved. That list would be far shorter.

So, what does this mean in practice? Employees are over-committed. They are asked to join more meetings, sit in on conference calls, attend presentations or network events and share knowledge in different settings. They belong to multiple project teams, which increases the diversity of their work, their leadership experience, and the volume of incoming e-mails. The most willing colleagues agree to share their knowledge in different forums and find themselves answering requests for information that in many cases could have been found in centrally stored project documentation.

It is at this point that fatigue or stress sets in as team members wonder where their responsibility starts and ends. They may feel concerned about missing important information if they reduce the number of meetings they attend. Job variety and increased involvement can be highly appealing, yet people's sense of work satisfaction can suffer when they discover they are lacking focus or effectiveness in doing their 'own' work.

I have noticed that many of my clients are absorbed by the word 'ownership'. They ask questions such as:

- Am I the owner of this additional project or am I an advisor?
- Do all these overlapping areas of expertise fall under my responsibility or am I the coordinator?
- Which meetings can I afford to skip?
- I find I am the one signing off on every development stage – does this make me the overall owner?
- How do I deal with this situation of unwritten horizontal or diagonal shared ownership?
- How many self-managed, cross-functional or fluid teams can I handle?

Leaders need to address these questions up front to prevent ongoing uncertainty.

Most senior leaders tend to encourage direct reports to be the overall 'owner' of cross-departmental projects. They like to know to whom they can go for accountability. Secondly, ownership in a leader's team can have a positive effect on the visibility and influence of their department. Does an employee hold sole or shared ownership? Is their involvement full cycle or limited to a project phase? Leaders need to step up and address these questions to safeguard the wellbeing and effectiveness of their teams.

How colleagues work together in businesses today has developed into an overload of co-operation. Teams have become overstretched and overcommitted, resulting in more stress and less time to share knowledge. So, where does the solution lie? In a different kind of team leadership and a supporting operating model.

Leaders have focused on bringing down barriers between departments and teams, but have not paid sufficient attention to creating the right conditions for productive co-operation in a highly-connected business environment. Behavioural changes, identifying bottlenecks and redefining roles and responsibilities are major parts of the solution, alongside monitoring of processes to facilitate effective co-operation. We'll refer to this again in Chapter Seven when we will discuss leadership of fluid teams.

Restrictive problem solving and decision making

Team processes have suffered due to the demand for broader co-operation, especially if workable team co-operation frameworks are missing. I will address two processes in this section: problem solving and decision making.

With employees' having to divide their limited time between multiple tasks and areas of responsibility, they are likely to agree to the quickest and easiest solution to problems that arise. If the solution is supported by the majority and does not require additional review meetings or the need to gain buy-in from other parties, it is considered good enough. And another issue can be ticked off the list as being resolved.

In many cases, these solutions are not the best that could have been reached. The quick-fix approach does not allow time for exploring members' ideas and original thoughts. Without proper processes in place, problem solving is reduced to trouble shooting. If problems are solved in a trouble-shooting manner, teams are guaranteed a steady flow of new problems.

TROUBLE SHOOTING VS PROBLEM SOLVING

When I met with a senior manager of an international research company recently, she told me that she had solved a problem that had arisen between two department heads. Both were in close contact with the same global account, and each thought they should chair the afternoon meeting with this client. The manager intervened and found a solution that would allow both department heads to manage the meeting in a balanced manner. She also arranged for a board member to welcome the client and open the meeting to ensure that neither department head took precedence over the other.

Although she felt pleased she had solved the problem efficiently, what she had in fact done was a bit of last-minute trouble shooting. Therefore, unclear expectations, vague lines of communication and unresolved responsibility or accountability issues would reoccur, only next time the problem could be more difficult to solve. Each piece of unresolved history adds to the burden of future conflicts.

If leaders don't address the core problem, teams are seriously limited in their progress and the work climate will suffer. One problem that is removed superficially simply makes room for another. In this regard, leading by example means addressing the cause, not fixing the consequence.

The second process that does not thrive in many teams today is decision making. People are faced with multiple priorities and rapid change, tighter deadlines, the availability of more data and a variety of readily available opinions. Mixed interests and loyalties may come into play if colleagues are in any way linked to each other's projects. It can be difficult to disagree with a member of Team A if that person's co-operation is required for results in Team B.

Individuals and teams require a decision-making process. If individuals do not have a process that describes in simple steps how they reach decisions, then other issues such as their moods, biases and experiences may become decisive factors.

Having a personal routine also ensures that team members know which phase of the decision-making process they are in. Only then can they act in accordance with what is expected in that phase. When circumstances instead of guiding processes drive decisions, the decision maker often informs or involves people too soon or too late, or involves the wrong people and overlooks others. Evidence of the over-involvement of people in certain stages is an excessive number of CC e-mails.

Poor problem solving can cause a team to lose its effectiveness and influence. Poor decision making can lead to a serious lack of trust. If trust is to be rebuilt, leaders need to improve transparency radically. This can only be achieved if decision-making formats, the choice of decision criteria and testing of assumptions become steps that are consciously and consistently taken.

A different kind of leader develops their own problem-solving and decision-making routines that withstand the disruptive impact of ongoing change. Teams, too, require a framework to help them solve problems and make decisions more effectively for improved productivity and profitability. Minor adjustments within existing procedures will not provide the level of change teams need to make today. It is time to look at the framework in which teams operate and replace restrictive approaches with new ones. Leaders need to facilitate this process.

The missing ingredient – empathy

As societies, predominantly in Western cultures, have become more individualistic, they have lost a degree of empathy.

According to social psychologist and professor at Maastricht University, Geert Hofstede, the top four most individualistic societies in the world are the USA, Australia, Great Britain and The Netherlands. In individualistic cultures, people see each other as only loosely connected, and are expected to look after themselves and their immediate families only. They place much more value on their personal goals and achievements than on the group's interests.

How does one recognise that empathy is lacking within teams and what is the consequence of this? First of all, not every team in individualistic societies will lack empathy. Neither can we say that all teams in collective societies will be highly empathetic. However, there is a connection between individualism and a lower level of empathy.

A lack of empathy is present when individuals do not understand or feel what another person is experiencing within that person's frame of reference. The ability to place oneself in another person's situation involves an understanding of their emotional state of mind. If a lack of empathy goes uncorrected and does not have a negative impact on people achieving personal ambitions, this may become engrained in how a team functions.

The consequences of teams lacking empathy are felt most in the work climate. Disagreements, frustrations and low trust levels characterise teams that lack empathy. A lack of transparency will likely increase, as will the number of people complaining about having to play the political game to succeed at work. There will typically be more monologues than dialogues, more 'Yes, but' responses than questions, and a win-lose approach during debates and conversations. The benefits of diversity will be lost. This has a limiting and costly effect on the quality of knowledge and experience shared between colleagues.

Those who take the lead in establishing gender, intercultural, intergenerational or neurological diversity within their organisations require the use of empathy as opposed to more rules and regulations to make it happen. For example, what can a leader do to ensure female talent is used more? Classical advice would be to enforce various measures, from new recruitment procedures to quotas, and to send staff on diversity courses. However, research confirms that none of these solutions will bring about sustainable change because they irritate the male majority, and high-potential women leaders are not in favour of stigmatising gender-related preferential treatment when applying for a top position.

What could you do to create a more level playing field in your organisation? Consider the power of using empathy to observe and act on gender dynamics. By identifying harsh behaviour or lack of kindness and addressing this, you show social connectedness.

The next step is to lead by example and demonstrate the value of women leaders. Consider replacing target quotas with assessing the extent to which gender equality and inclusion are applied by individuals on a day-to-day basis. That would be a different kind of performance measurement – one that is not rule based but behaviour based. Finding the loophole where rules are concerned is one thing, but having none to hide behind is quite another.

Cultural diversity thrives in environments where empathy is present. Empathy makes people want to learn about each other. If empathy is lacking, employees tend to ignore or criticise differences.

Most people can learn to develop empathy. What it will take for many is an understanding of the consequences of not valuing or applying this side of human behaviour. If employees consider the price of not changing high, change becomes more appealing. Secondly, rewarding employees for the right behaviour is likely to lead to a repeat, and slowly a new behavioural pattern is established.

Summary

Every manager wishes to have a team that is dynamic and effective. In this chapter, we addressed some of the dilemmas leaders face in their day-to-day interaction with their teams, zooming in on the most common circumstances that hinder team progress:

- The over-analysed and stereotyped team
- An overload of unchannelled co-operation
- Restrictive problem solving and decision making
- The missing ingredient: empathy

This would be a good time to reflect on limitations you have observed in teams within your organisation. Make a note of them and determine their impact.

Teams that are limited in their co-operation and development will not be prepared for accelerated change, disruption and the opportunities and challenges related to steeply increased global connectivity. Therefore, it is time to consider an attractive alternative. What this will take is a different kind of team leadership.

7

Modern Team and
Intergenerational Leadership

The strength of the team is each individual member.
The strength of each member is the team.
Phil Jackson

Leadership of fluid teams and intergenerational leadership are not only indispensable areas of expertise, I also consider them to be inseparable. They strengthen each other, and if one is missing, the other has little added value.

These are large topics to cover. The insights, considerations and practical examples I share will, therefore, not cover them in all-encompassing detail. I will describe what I believe are the most important ideas to facilitate the development of effective team and intergenerational leadership.

We will start by giving both topics separate attention to highlight the challenges and opportunities each one brings. We will then look at how a different kind of leader combines both leadership requirements.

Leadership of fluid teams

*Tell me and I forget. Teach me and I may
remember. Involve me and I learn.*
Benjamin Franklin

In what way are organisations transitioning from a focus
on traditional teams to self-managed teams? Should self-
management principles apply to the entire organisation?
How far should organisations go and what does this mean
for leaders? How should a leader manage employees who
are assigned to multiple projects simultaneously?

Teams are moving on from traditional formats. Leadership
of fluid teams is about effective leadership of teams that
are progressive, changing, multi-tasked and self-managed.
They are not permanent. They grow and shrink in different compositions to meet changing needs. They assemble
and disassemble depending on project requirements and
objectives. Fluid team building is a skill that leaders need
to develop to be able to assemble the talent needed for any
challenging new project or business venture.

Whatever phase your company may be in and regardless
of how you describe your teams, it is best to be prepared
for a fundamental change in how they function. Therefore,
the leadership principles that build resilient teams that are
open to change and diversity should be applied to virtually
all categories of teams. The competencies a leader builds
in this area can be used equally successfully to increase
the effectiveness of long-standing cross-functional teams.
Such teams may be less transitional than fluid teams, but
today they too require a high level of self-management and
diversity of talent. Leading fluid teams effectively is more

than a competency, it is a skill that will be indispensable for leaders in the years to come.

ENERGISING GROUPS

Something I have learned in my work in various countries is that cultures may be different, but certain interpersonal principles and experiences have an equally motivating effect on people both in flat and hierarchical organisations. My first confirmation of how certain business practices connect and energise people everywhere was in Bratislava. Before that, I had worked mainly in Western, Northern and Southern Europe.

I remember vividly how I was welcomed as the seminar leader and moderator to a technical institution. The conference room was elegant and stately. Fifteen smartly dressed middle-aged men sat at a long varnished wooden conference table. They represented divisions that worked independently of each other.

The Director's opening words were, 'Welcome to our country, Ms Poot. We do not need you to tell us to write our losses with a red pen or our profits with a green pen. If you have new and ground-breaking ideas for the real problems we face, you are welcome to stay and work with us.'

Well, this was a unique introduction! Much to my delight (not shown, of course), my response surprised the Director, in particular my statement that I was looking forward to sharing insights with his management team who would make their own choices. I was not there to teach, tell or demonstrate how things should be done. The Director then returned to his office and came back at the end of the day for a recap of the results.

What happened in between? For the first hour, all the gentlemen listened attentively, did not interact much, took notes, and replied rather reluctantly to questions only when prompted to do so. And then I divided the group into subgroups. There was no hierarchy in the room. The participants stood around flip charts and worked on business cases that were applicable to their circumstances. They brainstormed on outcomes that met the criteria they had set together. There was unrestrained chatter and enthusiasm.

The subsequent plenary sharing of the results of each group discussion was totally energising. Thanks to a sequential interpreter, I was fully aware of what the participants were saying and what resonated with the team most. By this time, they were answering my questions without hesitation, and each group was reaching interesting alternatives, possible solutions and conclusions. They even voluntarily drew pictures of what their future organisation could look like.

When the Director returned, I asked a volunteer from each group to present the outcome of their group's discussion. This was new, as usually the highest in rank would convey all messages to the Director. The Director was taken aback that we had deviated from this principle. He informed me that it was important to him to know who had said what. However, he sat down, listened to the speakers and concluded that we had been successful.

He heard things he had not heard before as each group presented their findings. The speakers weren't speaking on behalf of themselves or the highest in rank. They represented their group's ideas and perspectives, and this gave them noticeable presence and confidence. They had interacted with different colleagues in new team compositions, sharing ideas on future developments that would affect them all. Connection through relevant and active involvement raised their energy levels. This proved to me that leading differently to optimise involvement and motivation does not only work in flat organisations with loose lines of communication. This management team was used to hierarchical business practices, yet responded well to aspects of fluid team leadership.

If we fast-forward to the end of 2017, we arrive in Albania and Macedonia, where I led leadership programmes in the consultancy sector. Each of these countries' unique business cultures differs in their own way from the most prevalent business cultures in affluent economies in Western Europe. Again, I found that motivational drivers transcend borders, cultures, history, economic status and personal challenges. Active involvement and self-managed work groups have an empowering effect on people. Therefore, even if an organisation is not ready for fluid teams, the core principles of this new kind of leadership may prove to be the fastest way to achieve prosperity.

I believe all leaders need to endorse the principles of fluid team leadership:

- Modern team and network-driven organisations generate better results than organisations structured in traditional hierarchy and departmental silos
- Working with modern teams, i.e. fluid teams, requires a new or adapted operating model

The extent to which fluid team leadership is rolled out in any organisation will depend on the company's readiness to move to a more networked team structure. Company leaders choose which elements would be most valuable to their organisation and to which degree they wish to implement the principles of fluid leadership.

Principle 1: Modern teams and networks vs hierarchy and departmental silos. Current styles of communication, the power of social media and the increase in business across borders are eroding the effectiveness of traditional hierarchies. Teams are gaining more authority to interact with their counterparts in different regions. Interaction between teams is broader, deeper and faster than before, and this continues to shift real-time product or market knowledge from company leaders to lower ranking teams.

This is leading to significant changes in how teams work. It is becoming the norm that employees fulfil multiple roles. Team members gain a sense of gratification and influence when they are asked to join an additional (temporary) team where they may become a team leader thanks to their specific knowledge. They may join a third team as an advisor or person who contributes in a different way. Either way, they gain leadership experience and/or insights through broader-based participation. Learning is accelerated. Teams organise themselves by defining their purpose, their way of working and their individual roles and objectives. Peer-to-peer learning becomes a powerful tool for employees to upscale their skills. Team members, often uninhibited Millennials, do not shy away from contacting more highly ranked colleagues who may be experts in a field that concerns their project team. Consequently, traditional lines of communication make way for more horizontal and diagonal lines that shorten the distance to knowledge centres and sign-off power.

This swing towards a network-driven operation did not happen out of the blue. Increased global, intra-company and inter-company connectivity have facilitated broader collaboration. To put the connectivity increase in perspective, Cisco's Visual Networking Forecast (VNI) has projected that 4.1 billion people will be using the internet in 2020. Global internet traffic surpassed one zettabyte in 2017, which is equal to about one trillion gigabytes. By 2020, that figure will reach 2.3 zettabytes.

With both areas of communication expanding so rapidly, traditional departmental boundaries and silos cannot be maintained. However, anything that is not led or guided with a clearly defined purpose is not sustainable. If teams evolve in this manner and represent the beginning of a self-management operating model without parameters and the full support of the company's leaders, the benefits will be marginal. Above all, the risks of ineffective processes and overtaxed employees will weigh heavily on the organisation's productivity and profitability. Therefore, co-operation across product, functional and geographical lines must be coordinated effectively to mitigate these risks and stimulate growth. A new operating model will achieve this.

Principle 2: A new operating model. If a structure does not change to support operations, an organisation will become strategically slow. Much of a leader's energy will be directed at making processes work, pushing for improved internal efficiency and dealing with frictions. So, the question is not whether an organisation should adapt its operating model; the question is how and when.

Before leaders design a new operating model for modern teams, it is important to know which criteria it should meet and how leaders can prepare for the right kind of change. A guiding checklist is a helpful tool. The six criteria outlined below unlock talent from different pockets of the organisation and stimulate involvement across the board. Changes that support these criteria will be changes that prepare the organisation for modern-day transitions.

Checklist of six criteria that prepare organisations for modern-day transitions

Decisions and processes should support the following:

- **Increased team autonomy**
- **Cross-functional co-operation** is facilitated
- Employees can fulfil **different roles** based on their talents and expertise, and are not confined to standard job descriptions
- **Team diversity** is seen as an asset and stimulated
- There is **clarity and transparency** regarding processes, ownership and expectations, supported by modern communication tools
- Teams are in **closer contact** with clients

If operating models and day-to-day decisions support these criteria, the foundations will be in place to apply and build on self-management principles in a step-by-step process. Leaders will have the flexibility to decide on the measure in which self-management is applied throughout the organisation.

Research suggests that elements of self-organisation will be valuable to all organisations. Therefore, it is never too soon to establish a structure that will facilitate this new way of working to become more competitive and agile. However, certain hierarchical procedures are likely to retain a place in organisations. Without any hierarchy at all, the measurable benefits of fluid teams will be disappointing.

So, what does a transformed operating model suited to current business developments mean in practice? As a starting point, certain tools and procedures engrained in businesses across the globe will be reshaped or replaced. Organisations with modern operating models are likely to work according to the following principles:

Job descriptions become obsolete. Employees' identities are not narrowly defined by their positions and authority. Professional identities evolve based on the roles employees fulfil and their added value. Leaders and employees agree on the required skills for certain roles and role-related objectives as opposed to a standardised job description.

Appraisals are as dynamic as the teams themselves. Frequent dialogue on progress, achievements in different roles, objectives and experiences replaces the predictable format of appraisal meetings that may be archaic, subjective and reactive. Appraisals are no longer the exclusive domain of hierarchical work relationships. Reviews and evaluations on a peer-to-peer level expedite learning and self-awareness.

Redefining high potentials. Who are they? Company management reassesses from time to time what makes an employee in their organisation a high-potential individual. They may use external professionals to fine-tune this process. Which talents are required? Which behaviour matters most?

If, for example, the existing criteria used to identify high potentials are related almost exclusively to productivity, this could breed a culture that puts volume above innovation. The highest potentials may be those most highly engaged and committed to progress.

Modernised reward systems. Employee rewards are upgraded to include achievements in more than one role and behaviour that furthers the organisation's overall performance. What a company rewards is what a company will get. If bottom-line results are rewarded so highly that all other contributions become optional extras, then management will be paying lip service to the very behaviour that is needed to sustain growth, a healthy work climate and ongoing development.

Adapted communication styles. Streamlined communication is oxygen for fluid teams and modern operating models. Communication guidelines need to be defined and shared within the organisation. The leader's example is vital in ensuring that effective brevity becomes the norm. Leaders upgrade their communication skills and switch between communication styles so that their messages resonate with their audiences. Messages have a core statement communicated with clarity to inform/motivate/involve/persuade etc. Internal e-mails are heavily restricted and replaced with tools that create dialogue involving the right people for the right reasons.

Communication tools build a united culture. Services such as Skype or Google Hangouts enhance communication between colleagues in remote teams, and between all parties in the 'open workforce'. Encouraging informal communication between colleagues is a vital aspect of building a healthy work climate and inclusive environment that foster a sense of belonging.

Non-traditional meetings. Time-consuming traditional meetings are replaced by personal or video meetings. Participation and contributions are role related, which increases the relevance of the meetings for each participant. Agendas are dynamic and aimed to engage all present. Most meetings are led by fluid team heads, not departmental heads. Opportunities, strategic choices, project achievements and accountability related to objectives are key drivers for all face-to-face or remote meetings.

Technology and team discipline. Up-to-date technology is required to ensure developments are documented and information is updated regularly. All qualitative and quantitative data needs to be stored where it is accessible to all concerned, which requires discipline founded on mutual interdependency. This quick and easy access to relevant knowledge becomes an organisation's greatest competitive advantage.

Codified and tacit knowledge. Codified knowledge is explicit and can be documented. Tacit knowledge is implicit, mainly experience-based, and is more difficult to transfer. It can, however, be captured when the knowledge holder provides mentoring or allows job shadowing. Other methods include online collaborative platforms and structural recording of lessons learned. This enhances the value of debriefing sessions after projects. Rapid knowledge sharing leads to shorter response times to all stakeholders. Capitalising on the value of tacit knowledge may be one of the most challenging objectives organisations strive to achieve, but it is certainly one of the most rewarding.

Customer focus vs reciprocation. When organisations become more inwardly focused, complex or politicised, reciprocation can become part of how individuals work together – you scratch my back and I'll scratch yours. Leaders need to discourage reciprocation in modern organisation models and fluid teams. A team member's contribution in team A should not entail a colleague returning special favours when both are involved in team B. Neither should it guarantee the team member a more senior role in a different project team. If teams put the interests of the customer and the talents and expertise required for each project centre stage, attention shifts from personal gains to personal growth, the latter being the more motivational of the two.

To meet the criteria outlined in the checklist, operating models will require a formalised agreement on the way of working.

Modern teams thrive on fluidity, accelerated learning, members belonging to more than one team, close contact with clients, and a spirit that drives progress. A framework to serve this model is what separates progressive leaders from traditional leaders. This is where disruption is handled with more aptitude and teams become agile, reliable and engaged.

My recommendation is for company leaders to form a task force to create this framework, setting out how fluid teams are created and how they should operate after identifying their purpose and requirements. This task force will review progress and bottlenecks to ensure talents are used competently and not in a way that limits knowledge sharing, creative progress and personal development. Allocating the right members to teams, achieving beneficial diversity, methods to determine the scope of different roles, and guidelines for communication within and between teams, are all fundamental elements that lay the foundations for teams to manage themselves well. Leadership lies within the teams themselves. It is rooted in different roles. Shorter communication lines and a market-driven approach put employees in every process in personal and purposeful contact with clients. There is a level of hierarchy within the teams, but as this hierarchy is attached to a person's role (e.g. team leader or process manager) rather than individuals, more employees gain leadership experience and decision-making responsibility.

An example of an advanced form of self-organisation is holacracy. The Holacracy Operating Model was developed by HolacracyOne LLC. It specifies governance and operational processes to maximise transparency, effectiveness, action and innovation. The holacracy constitution that defines this self-management model can be accessed via the holacracy.org website.

As holacracy is an advanced form of self-organisation, it would be a bridge too far for many companies. It is thought-provoking, however, to see how a range of mainly US based companies is adopting different operating models that radically change how people work together to drive innovation.

A manageable and yet significant step forward would be the removal of barriers that currently block any of the six criteria required for fluid teams. Then open the door to cross product, functional and geographical team work, and ensure a framework is in place to safeguard the evolvement of such teams. Dynamic team work that ticks the boxes of the six criteria will become contagious, leading to new achievements and a highly-engaged workforce. A new operating model then takes shape that delivers a greater competitive advantage and better revenues.

Intergenerational leadership

It is not our differences that divide us.
It is our inability to recognise, accept
and celebrate those differences.
Audre Lorde

RESPECT

The dirt road continues for miles; the air is hot and dry. Children come skipping down the road playing with sticks and a tyre. They run barefoot towards a group of women who have gathered at a borehole. This gated borehole sinks to a depth of 50 metres to reach an abundance of crystal-clear, healthy drinking water.

Where are we? In rural South Africa where I initiated a charity project to give 35,000 people access to clean drinking water. Once water diviners had found deep ground water, they determined the exact locations of the future boreholes. The chief of each community decided on the sequence in which they would be sunk. High fencing around each of the twenty boreholes safeguarded the taps and other surface components from 'disappearing'. The gate was opened at sunrise, by which time blue, yellow and white jerry cans were lined up, indicating the order in which the women would use the taps. The gate was locked again before sunset.

Who was given responsibility for the key to the borehole? The gatekeeper would have to be the most highly respected person in the community. Who would this person be? The most vocal or popular man? A strong person between thirty and forty? The chief's nephew? The local schoolteacher who knew all the families?

None of the above. In keeping with tribal custom, this honour was granted to the oldest person in the community.

While the group of women talked and disciplined their children at the borehole, a very bent elderly lady arrived with a large key in her hand. She was greeted with warmth and enthusiasm. After saying a few words in Zulu, she proudly unlocked the gate. Before long, women were walking away from the borehole with 20 litre jerry cans on their heads. The old lady sat on a chair in the shade of a nearby tree, looking satisfied as people came and went.

This is an example of the philosophy of 'Ubuntu', meaning 'humanity towards others'. The core of Ubuntu is captured in the principle: 'I am what I am because of who we all are'. It is this deeper understanding of the needs and responsibilities of individuals, generations and entire communities that helps leaders to identify people's added value and to give a meaningful purpose to it.

Companies that struggle most to achieve effective diversity are those that do not have a guiding philosophy that underscores the unique value of different generations. If there are no guiding principles in place, company management will tend to speak of their organisation's open-minded work culture. The staff is described as an easy-going, unbiased workforce that sorts out differences among themselves. This may sound attractive and mature, but I have discovered that in any medium to large size company, it is usually a sign of leadership complacency. It is easier to call on the maturity of others than to take the lead in creating new circumstances that are most beneficial to the organisation's greatest asset: a diverse, progressive and effective workforce.

If senior management speaks of inter-company tolerance of differences, mistakes and opposing opinions as an asset, dig a little deeper. Tolerance is not a policy or a building block for company progress. If, on the other hand, leaders speak of business practices that suggest there is advanced inter-generational co-operation, that would indicate a proactive approach to benefiting from differences.

Understanding the differences

Multigenerational environments are prone to lack of under-standing and friction. As each generation has its own work ethics and communication preferences, styles will be different and will sometimes clash.

Let's take a look at a few areas where the differences between generations are most apparent.

Communication. Although all generations in the workforce have adopted the use of new technology, it is how they use it that sets them apart. Older employees are more likely to pick up the phone more frequently than their younger colleagues. Millennials will seek to make appointments, solve problems, acquire information and connect with others predominantly by using all the electronic options available to them. Expressions, choice of words, length of sentences and attention to grammar and context differ significantly between each generation.

And what about skills such as listening, questioning, nego-tiating, empathising? Older employees have been building on these skills throughout the many years of their careers. In nearly all circumstances, Millennials will apply informal communication with less variation in their styles.

Millennials may be seen as having a short attention span due to their fast-paced and multi-tasking work approach. They appreciate direct speech above detailed explanations and drawn out messages. Traditionalists and a high percentage of Baby Boomers will communicate from a viewpoint of respect for rules and structures. Generation X will enjoy challenging others and will feel comfortable being the devil's advocate in conversations. They do not like the use of jargon and clichés.

Meetings. Traditionalists, Baby Boomers and Generation Xers all appreciate face-to-face meetings, but each of these generations has a different motive for participating in meetings. The motives range from wanting to ensure responsibility has been taken for action points to wishing to be involved in decision making and seeking to obtain information that could not be submitted via any other channel. Millennials don't see the point of structured and mundane meetings, but meetings that bring them closer to achieving their objectives pass their test. They will want interaction, variation and to feel the relevance of their presence. Like younger Generation Xers, they will come prepared to multitask during a meeting in case it does not engage them. They do not consider working on their tablets and texting during meetings to be rude.

Traditionalists are accepting of the boss doing most of the talking. Traditionalists and Baby Boomers will also be accepting of an action list-driven meeting. This does not apply to Millennials, who disengage if hierarchy in the meeting leads to delays, repetitive arguments or lack of joint decision making. If the meeting does not require face-to-face communication, they consider their participation a waste of time. A web-based brainstorming session is likely to stimulate the Millennial more than a diluted form of knowledge sharing in a traditional meeting format.

Learning. Contrary to stereotypical views that imply older employees are less willing to learn, research suggests that employees in all generation brackets are keen to learn. Statistics show that employees in their fifties receive a fraction of the number of training hours given to younger employees. This is indicative of an organisation's priorities and has no reflection on the willingness of each generation to gain new knowledge, experience and skills.

There is a difference, however, with regard to expectations of learning opportunities. Baby Boomers will appreciate the training investment they receive, Generation Xers will be more demanding in this area, and Millennials will consider training a non-negotiable condition for them to remain on board.

There are differences, too, in how the generations like to learn. Younger employees have grown up using multiple devices and platforms. Would this, therefore, mean that older generations are more comfortable with training based on personal interaction and younger generations appreciate interactive training delivered digitally to fit into their work patterns? Yes, although only to a certain extent. I have discovered in my work that all generations enjoy a blended form of learning, i.e. both face-to-face training (bricks-and-mortar based) and training via an online platform. Gaining knowledge through different methods that offer variation and flexibility enables employees to learn in a way most suited to their needs. This accelerates learning throughout the organisation.

These different methods are not restricted to a trainer in a classroom or animated online modules. More imagination is required than this. A variety of tools in each category could include short lectures, mentoring, discussion groups, courses on-site, peer-to-peer group case studies, and web-based dialogue and interactive video.

And then we have the use of technology itself. Older employees will take a different approach to learning to use new technology. This process may come to them less intuitively than it does to Millennials, but they will learn more diligently and are less likely to forget certain features and benefits.

Opportunities for leaders

The differences between the generations bring opportunities and accelerated progress if a leader capitalises on them. In practical terms, the leader needs to embrace an approach that involves seeing differences, looking for unique values in each generation within the organisation and identifying knowledge gaps. The leader will discover a possible lack of diversity in both thought and approach or a need to upscale skills to match external challenges. Every inadequacy that comes to light provides the opportunity to make a difference.

The role of the leader goes beyond encouraging cross-generational teams. It entails designing a framework that is based on teams being cross-generational.

Some practical examples:

- Imagine how powerful it would be if Baby Boomers were involved in navigating politically charged environments prior to the organisation strategising the group's position and what they offer.

- Millennials complement every group with their ability to think in short sentences and produce the brevity required for a faster paced environment. They are indispensable in study groups seeking new ways to assess and influence a target group's preferences.

• It takes a dedicated team to achieve a positive work climate for all. Generation Xers' involvement in achieving a friendly, open and informal work climate can bring a sense of belonging to a geographically dispersed workforce. But without the involvement of Millennials in designing work processes, fun would be lacking from the fast-paced work environment and Millennials need both pace and fun to thrive.

Should choosing new technology be assigned to younger Generation Xers and Millennials? If older generations are also part of the team, they will look beyond the novel features of the technology and question its benefits and how it will increase productivity.

Some of the most inspirational mutual learning experiences take place in cross-generational teams. These are the teams that should be given responsibility for defining the most appropriate messages for diverse stakeholders and linking them to cutting-edge visual materials. And picture the benefit of a cross-generational team preparing for top-level negotiations. The older generations will usually bring a mix of priceless wisdom and tenacity, negotiation insights and patience. Millennials will bring new and innovative ideas. What better combination to determine the bottom-line alternatives if an agreement is not reached?

If a leader is aware of the different preferences and the unique value of each generation in the organisation, these differences can be used to modernise processes such as dealing with conflicts, giving feedback, decision making and knowledge sharing. Modernised processes enable organisations to become more agile. A second significant benefit is that organisations achieve a better balance in providing appropriate ongoing learning experiences tailored to the needs of each generation.

And what will help the leader to implement the changes? Persuasion? Charismatic influence? Perseverance? Those would be useful qualities, but they will not provide sustainable progress. What it will take is change by design. Designing the right framework to facilitate progress through advanced team work and intergenerational synergy will bring sustainable change.

As examples of change by design, there are Millennial mentorship programmes that are slowly but steadily gaining ground in the corporate world. This is most noticeable in American companies where executives are paired with junior employees who share tech knowledge and bring different perspectives to marketing the organisation's products and services. Executives report that these sessions with Millennials are inspiring and help them connect with their future markets. Millennials are cognizant of phenomena such as vlogging. With some video blogs having over 100 million subscribers, they have immense influence over what young consumers buy. This form of reversed mentoring has proven to save companies vast sums of money that would otherwise be spent on generational advice sourced from external consultants.

It takes a conscious choice to lead a workforce that outperforms its competitors thanks to generational diversity. It requires a system anchored in procedures that make diversity an added value, not an obligation, and facilitate how teams work together. This is where proactive leadership of fluid teams and intergenerational leadership come together. Both require separate attention to identify opportunities and remove barriers, but a basic framework of co-operation facilitates both.

Leadership today is about combining the application of insights with the formalisation of new practices. There is no time like the present to adapt your role as a leader of a multigenerational workforce.

Summary

This chapter was devoted to one of a leader's greatest challenges: to provide team leadership that increases an organisation's agility, competitiveness and productivity. It is this kind of leadership that differentiates progressive leaders from traditional leaders. We discussed in practical terms the meaning of the golden combination of modern team and intergenerational leadership.

Starting with modern team leadership, we discussed the two principles on which it is based:

- Fluid teams and network-driven organisations generate better results than organisations structured in traditional hierarchy and departmental silos
- Working with fluid teams requires a new or adapted operating model

You gained knowledge of the six criteria checklist. If all organisational and procedural changes meet these criteria, an organisation will build agility, competitiveness and productivity.

We then looked at intergenerational leadership, looking at several differences between the generations and how to turn these differences into synergy. By creating a framework that supports both fluid and cross-generational teams, leaders provide the circumstances and guiding principles to ensure change is sustainable and teams prosper in self-managed structures. This framework makes cross-generational teams a welcome given, not an option.

I recommend you take time to reflect before answering the following questions, and you may like to include personal notes.

Nurturing intergenerational teams

KEY QUESTIONS THAT HIGHLIGHT OPPORTUNITIES
Does your organisation have a widely-supported philosophy regarding intergenerational co-operation?
Would you call yourself a leader who uses generational diversity as a tool to maximise business results and knowledge sharing?
To what extent have you facilitated team co-operation beyond product, departmental or geographical borders?
Have you given thought to each generation's added value and how best to utilise it?
Page through this chapter and choose insights that you intend to implement. Which are they?

This table can be downloaded at http://www.jpcint.com/publications

Change can be challenging; foreseen and unforeseen resistances are part of the journey to rewarding results. In the next chapter, we will discuss what you can do to sustain progress and momentum.

8

When the Going Gets Tough

I have not failed,
I've just found 10,000 ways that won't work.
Thomas A. Edison, inventor of the light bulb

As a leader, your position may be lonely and things will not always go your way. There will be tough times and setbacks, disappointments and frustration. The measure of your success will be how you respond to setbacks or failure.

Fatigue, lack of enjoyment and a sense that you do not have matters sufficiently under control are likely to have a negative impact on your creativity and effectiveness. These feelings can lead to a loss of momentum, and it is in that vacuum that you may become vulnerable to uncertainty and distraction. If you doubt your choices, you may also lose your sense of achievement and progress. Because these situations are unavoidable in our current business climate, I am dedicating this final chapter to how to cope effectively.

We will start with some magic potion: building and sustaining momentum.

Momentum – what is it and how do you build it?

Used metaphorically, momentum refers to something being on a roll and gaining strength as it moves. It implies impetus, energy and progress. Excitement happens at the beginning of a project or idea. Momentum, on the other hand, comes later, as the project progresses or the idea is implemented. It starts with successful endings and thrives on next steps. Therefore, to energise ourselves and others, to make change easier and enhance performance, we need to give priority to building and maintaining momentum.

Guiding principles

Make personal choices and stick to them. Staying on track and building momentum on a day-to-day basis requires commitment.

When you read the previous chapters, did you highlight areas you intend to focus on? If so, prioritise these and select areas you will work on first. Ensure that you pay conscious attention to these every day, even if just for fifteen minutes. Frequency of execution is far more important than duration to generate the momentum needed for progress. Frequency builds consistency, credibility and skill.

Do not blame anyone for mistakes or a mediocre performance. Reflect on the developments and circumstances that led to the setback and find a way to turn it into a lesson. By sharing the lesson, you will use it proactively to teach others as opposed to being the reactive victim of circumstance. This attitude prevents a setback from stalling momentum.

Listen, test assumptions and ask questions. This will enable you to gain a thorough understanding of the situation causing confusion or affecting employee morale. Stay at it, connect with others and show involvement. Take the time you need to achieve sound decision making. This spreads confidence. Stay clear of the temptation to dive into troubleshooting mode. Nothing erodes the responsibility of others more quickly than a leader fixing their problems for them.

Create a positive, productive and happy environment. The leader needs to project optimism and see situations from different perspectives to generate an optimistic atmosphere, even when the going gets tough. This should be a top priority, together with policies that stimulate a happy, friendly work climate. This will build the buffer needed when turbulence puts both your and your team's resilience to the test.

Keep the flow going. Momentum grows with new opportunities. Ongoing development and progress need next steps. Achieving a goal without speaking of how it makes the next step possible will discourage those who are driven by improvement and innovation. Help others to visualise future benefits every time a milestone is reached.

When change becomes overwhelming

In this digital world of disruption, leaders can struggle to cope with all the changes that are either initiated by design or simply happen as a result of ongoing technological advancement. Leaders tend to believe that they need to be the drivers of change and join the ranks of the most visionary, showing the way to employees in different departments and markets. This, however, can lead to stress. No leader can stay abreast of all technological developments and use all social media platforms intensively enough to remain up to date.

Old school 'change management' books described step-by-step procedures that led to successful change. Those procedures worked well in times of stability and in more hierarchical organisational structures. However, some of the key principles are less applicable today. For example, change does not always start at the top and there is too much emphasis on people's natural resistance to change.

Our world has changed, and so must a leader's approach. Change can no longer be managed.

On a recent trip to Germany, I stayed at a beautiful country hotel set in the wooded hills of the Northern Eifel district. The reading table was decked with a range of German magazines. I chose to read one of them, *Manager Seminare, das Weiterbildungsmagazine,* that contained an article written by Dr Hans-Jaochim Gergs, lecturer at the Executive Education Center of the TU München and the University of Heidelberg. In his article, Dr Gergs listed the myths of change management.

He debunks the longstanding belief that a crisis or urgency is required to achieve change. On the contrary, Dr Gergs explains how excitement for future opportunity is the engine that drives attractive change. Employees who not only learn what they need to know for their day-to-day work, but are also given the opportunity to learn and develop in other areas see opportunities that they had not identified before. Not a deficit, but a surplus of financial means, talent and know-how allow a company to experiment, and this lays the foundation for successful and ongoing change.

Therefore, the premise that people require a crisis or an amplified sense of urgency to accept change is outdated. Dr Gergs quotes the American organisational expert, Peter Senge: 'People do not resist change, they resist being changed.' This more positive approach suggests that employees like working for organisations that stay ahead of developments and reward creativity. Change is part of this business lifestyle.

This reminds me of extensive research that was conducted some years ago into what motivates people most. The outcome of that survey, conducted in the USA and spanning continents, was progress. Progress does not come without change. Senior management, therefore, need to pay more attention to painting a picture of attractive future scenarios to engage people instead of strategising first to counteract resistance to change.

Another myth Dr Gergs shared with his readers is that fundamental change processes should be initiated and implemented from the top of an organisation. This is no longer feasible. Valuable change needs to be initiated at lower levels, too. His statement that 'People support what they create' underscores the value of modern organisational structures and teams. Change communities become the driver of innovative ideas.

What does this mean for a different kind of leader? The question for managers today is not 'How should change processes be managed?' but 'How to build an organisation that continually renews itself?' Dr Gergs sums it up well: 'Leaders should no longer see themselves as initiators, drivers and owners of change but as architects of an infrastructure that supports ongoing change.'

When change becomes overwhelming, ask yourself if you and your most senior colleagues are trying to manage change processes. If so, it is time to let go. Change initiatives no longer have a beginning and an end. They evolve into more change. Therefore, position yourself in the appropriate role where you create the right circumstances for continued modernisation and momentum. I believe that applying this perspective will help you to alleviate the pressure on you and members of your management team.

When opposition mounts

Expect detours

There is no short cut to creating something new, influencing others, introducing new work processes or merging two corporate cultures. Being prepared to invest more time in activities that build support should be part of the plan. Don't let disagreement take you by surprise as it is highly predictable in any situation where a lack of clarity can stimulate fear or cynicism. If it is ignored, it has the potential to become a distraction that ultimately results in a road block. It is at this point that disappointment or frustration sets in while you make energy draining attempts to persuade sceptics to get on board. Opposition is not bad luck, but an opportunity to understand its origins and find a better way to build more trustworthy support. A straight line to success may end up being the slow route, whereas accepting a few bends in the road is likely to bring results sooner.

Create a list of potential risks

If an idea or recommendation that you have made does not generate the level of support you had expected, you may find yourself defending your point of view. This undermines the value of any creative idea or plan. At this point, it is best to go to the drawing board and think about the objections, critical questions and opposition you may receive from each stakeholder. It does not take long to create a risk mitigation table. List your stakeholders in the first column, the behavioural risks in the middle column, and in the third column the actions you could take to mitigate each potential risk.

Taking proactive steps to discuss the possible causes of concern or doubt ensures that the risks are reduced. This also gives you vital and timely knowledge of the agendas, concerns and interests to be considered early on.

Reconnect based on curiosity

If you skipped the steps above and find yourself facing considerable opposition, then connect immediately with those opposing you to gain a better understanding of their objections. Identify the objections and work on building rapport. This will enable you to enter a dialogue with an enquiring mind as opposed to being intent on persuasion and winning an argument. Be patient and listen.

Reframe your message and approach

This is a fundamental requirement, if not condition, for others to (re)consider the short- and long-term benefits of your proposal. Presenting the same story, this time either more forcefully or with more tact, in a friendlier manner or as a team player, will be helpful but will not change the minds of those you are wanting to convince. You may require compromise or consideration of a third alternative. In any case, rework your proposal to include changes. Then reframe how you present it. A win-win requires a different story to sell the improved plan.

Increase your presence and communication

Ensure you remain visible and communicative. Under-communicating will widen the gap of understanding and respect between you and the sceptics. Use all the channels available to you for formal and informal communication so that your message reaches the recipients in the most effective format.

By avoiding your opponents, you will strengthen their resolve and facilitate the emergence of group resistance. Once you have engaged with them, determine at what point you have listened and responded sufficiently and have adequate support to proceed towards your goal.

Accept that you have supporters and opponents

There are those who drive processes and those who wait to be convinced. Progress is not built on keeping everyone happy, being popular or pleasing your adversaries. Following a transparent, fair and respectful process as described in Chapter Five will give you the confidence to recognise when it is time to move on. Maintaining momentum requires that you shift your attention back to those who are keen to accelerate. Remember that momentum does not wait. Neither do ambitious high potentials wait for everyone to catch up. By establishing an environment of continuous improvement, you allow the fastest group to set the pace, not those who stall progress.

Using your personal reset button

I consider building mental and physical resilience a priority for every leader. To retain their focus and positive energy during difficult times, leaders must be able to rely on a safety net. This safety net is a reset button to be used when the going gets tough.

Building resilience starts with the mindset that a leader's personal wellbeing is an integral part of their professional lives. Being fit and performing well professionally are complementary, mutually beneficial activities. If working on one's resilience is reserved for a day off or annual holiday, it will become a competing activity. Resilience will be depleted, not strengthened. We need more harmony between these activities, which means they need to overlap.

Understand what gives you energy and drains your energy. Make a list of the circumstances or patterns that belong in either the energy boost column or the energy draining column, then add what effect each activity has on you and areas of your performance. Building resilience is about using the positive column to enhance your performance and knowing how best to respond to activities in the negative column.

Do not accept that certain circumstances erode your effectiveness or undermine your professionalism in public. One of the foundations of personal development is learning to recognise and prepare for challenges which lie ahead. The tell-tale signs of potential difficulties are usually there, but are often ignored.

Being aware of people's behaviour, their style of communication and the dynamics of any setting is a skill that helps you to size up those around you. Tailoring your response to unexpected circumstances will come more easily if you are not fixated on the best possible outcome. By being better prepared for possible reactions from others, you will build variation in your repertoire of appropriate responses. This will help you to replace negative emotions or impulsive reactions with a compelling statement, question or explanation.

Tailoring your response means modifying your choice of words, switching to a different communication style and using your conduct and body language to strengthen your resolve or emphasise a receptive state of mind.

Reflect, Record, Rehearse, Remember, Reproduce

Do you sometimes regret that you were not able to respond with self-control and firmness when confronted with a totally unacceptable remark, accusation or request? Were you too accepting, diplomatic, quiet, frustrated, emotional, defensive or combative? Although you would not be the only person to struggle at such times, do not accept this shortcoming. Instead, Reflect on what happened. Think of what you would like to have said to make an impression you would have been proud of. Record the improved version, Rehearse it, Remember it, and be prepared to Reproduce it next time you find yourself in a similar situation.

When we're preparing for tough circumstances, we need to consider the worst-case scenario and have a response ready should it occur. Spontaneity is not always as spontaneous as people may think. Those who excel in dealing with the unexpected professionally, or who break the ice when atmospheres become tense, will most probably be drawing on experience and rehearsed responses. Planning to be spontaneous can be very smart.

Red flags

Recognising the circumstances that trigger negative emotions requires a heightened awareness of your personal red flags. Dealing effectively with these red flags requires knowledge of what helps you to retain a professional demeanour and deliver an exemplary response when it matters most.

Red flags are warning signals that you have left your comfort zone and are moving into a situation that normally triggers a negative response. They do not warrant poor behaviour or avoidance of the situation at hand. Rather, they forewarn you to prepare for an imminent discomfort by choosing how to respond. Press your reset button and use a response that will build your confidence and give you the edge on those who do not prepare for unexpected or undesirable situations.

These are experiences that are worth sharing with colleagues. Your response as a leader and the lessons you've learned build knowledge and engagement within teams.

Retain your professional conduct

Opinions are divided as to how much vulnerability a leader may show when pressures mount. Some employees are said to enjoy working for managers who publicly show their weakness. Management books refer to the leadership skill of showing one's vulnerability.

One of my clients told me that he had advised his commercial director, who was relocating to Mexico, to show his vulnerability. He believed this would help the Director to connect with the sales team on a personal level. My client's advice included the example of the Director openly sharing with his team that he had had a bad day. In fact, he even felt it would be OK for the commercial director to use a four-letter word to describe a tough meeting.

I advise you not to attach value to this point of view. Employees may lend an ear, but based on my experience listening to both executives and their direct reports in different cultures, I have no doubt that employees prefer to report to someone who is decisive, confident, energetic and resourceful. Most employees will experience the leader offloading negative emotions on to them to be a burden.

It is best to share your concerns, frustration or sense of help-lessness with those further removed from your immediate working environment. Nothing spreads through an organi-sation faster than emotion. Why confuse your environment by spreading negative energy one day and expecting every-one to be highly motivated by the next? Having to resort to four-letter words is a clear indication that circumstances control you. Reset to your professional self or remove your-self from the business setting to regroup.

Summary

It is easy to flourish in times of growth, support and pop-ularity. It is a lot tougher to retain a positive outlook and personal effectiveness when circumstances become con-frontational or hostile and team morale or business results take a nosedive. When these situations occur, multiple problems emerge.

As a leader, always be aware of the example that you give to others. Train yourself to build resilience when the going gets tough. Creating the best circumstances for progress is about building and sustaining momentum.

We discussed how to respond to change when it becomes overwhelming. Here, I emphasised the role of leaders as facilitators of change. Dealing with mounting opposition was the third section of this chapter, where I shared six practical recommendations with you.

Finally, I zoomed in on the importance of having a personal reset button to help you retain your composure and learn from mistakes and negative responses. This personal safety net helps you to do better next time and reduce the number of red flags you encounter in your senior role. The **R**eflect, **R**ecord, **R**ehearse, **R**emember, **R**eproduce model is sure to help you.

The personal reset button includes retaining a professional image regardless of one's thoughts or emotions. This is what sets forward-thinking leaders apart from task-driven managers in times of heightened stress.

Postscript

There is no better time than the present to follow through on your ideas to change patterns and apply a new approach. This world of disruption is a multidimensional world. Many aspects of the external and internal environment have an impact on our professional lives. These aspects do not come one at a time but accelerate simultaneously, which has changed the dynamics of our surroundings. Therefore, effective leadership today is about applying a multidimensional approach. To succeed, you need more than one plan.

It is for this reason that I encourage you to take decisive steps in more than one area and use the tips I have shared with you to achieve support for the changes you set in motion. The priorities you have highlighted throughout this book are the areas on which to focus.

This need not be a daunting process. On the contrary, establishing an environment of continuous improvement is energising. Applying the Kaizen approach may prove to be of value to you – Kaizen is a Japanese word meaning continuous improvement. The concept is that taking small steps on a regular basis will lead to large improvements over time.

If you wait for circumstances to be perfect before you initiate change in how you lead, you will lose opportunity. Perfection is not important, progress is. Some insights may be easier to implement than others. If you are hesitant regarding any change you wish to bring about, I have good news for you. My colleagues and I design tailor-made workshops and lectures for every topic that I have addressed in this book. Please contact me at j.poot@jpcint.com or visit our website at www.jpcint.com for further details.

It has been a pleasure writing for you.

Acknowledgements

My special thanks go to my mother who inspired me to write. She is a talented writer and has always been a great source of love and support as my number one fan.

I am indebted to my sister Caroline for being my sounding board for every chapter. Our conversations were encouraging and added joy to my writing. My thanks also go to Bart van der Heijden for generously accepting my request to write the foreword and to Lana van der Spiegel-Breytenbach for her preface.

I thank Joe Gregory, Managing Publisher, and Lucy McCarraher, Managing Editor, and their team at Rethink Press for their excellent support resulting in the publication of my book.

Last but not least, I thank all my clients for choosing to work with me. Every assignment in every setting has been memorable and laid the groundwork for this book. There can be no greater compliment than our ongoing co-operation in this world of disruption.

The Author

Janet Poot is an international busi-ness coach. She is originally from South Africa and currently lives in the Netherlands.

In writing *A Different Kind of Leader* she has drawn on years of experience as a marketing entrepreneur and subsequently as a leadership consultant with a range of mul-tinational clients. Her intercultural leadership experience in different markets, cultures and industries revealed to her that leaders in all geographical areas face similar challenges today. She designs leadership programmes, leads workshops in different countries, writes, and enjoys speaking to audi-ences to inspire a new role and approach for leaders.

To find out more about Janet and her work, visit her website
WEB http://www.jpcint.com/
in linkedin.com/in/janetpoot
@ADiffKindLeader

www.ingramcontent.com/pod-product-compliance
Lightning Source LLC
Chambersburg PA
CBHW072308210326
41519CB00057B/3094